NOVEL NOTES

Jerome K. Jerome

WITH ILLUSTRATIONS BY
J. GÜLICH, A. S. BOYD, HAL HURST, LOUIS WAIN,
GEO. HUTCHINSON, MISS HAMMOND,
J. GREIG, AND OTHERS

ALAN SUTTON

TO
BIG-HEARTED, BIG-SOULED, BIG-BODIED
FRIEND
CONAN DOYLE

ALAN SUTTON PUBLISHING LIMITED
PHOENIX MILL · FAR THRUPP · STROUD · GLOUCESTERSHIRE

ALAN SUTTON PUBLISHING INC
WOLFEBORO FALLS · NH 03896-0848

First published 1893

British Library Cataloguing in Publication data

Jerome, Jerome K. (Jerome Klapka) *1859–1927*
Novel notes.
1. English prose. Humorous prose
I. Title
828.91409

ISBN 0-86299-923-5

Library of Congress Cataloging in Publication data
applied for

Cover illustration: The Print Seller (*photograph: Fine Art Photographic
Library Ltd*)

Typesetting and origination by
Alan Sutton Publishing Limited.
Typeset in Imprint 10/11.
Printed in Great Britain by
The Guernsey Press Company Limited,
Guernsey, Channel Islands.

PROLOGUE

Years ago, when I was very small, we lived in a great house in a long, straight, brown-coloured street, in the east end of London. It was a noisy, crowded street in the daytime; but a silent, lonesome street at night, when the gas-lights, few and far between, partook of the character of lighthouses rather than of illuminants, and the tramp, tramp of the policeman on his long beat seemed to be ever drawing nearer, or fading away, except for brief moments when the footsteps ceased, as he paused to rattle a door or window, or to flash his lantern into some dark passage leading down towards the river.

The house had many advantages, so my father would explain to friends who expressed surprise at his choosing such a residence, and among these was included in my own small morbid mind the circumstance that its back windows commanded an uninterrupted view of an ancient and much-peopled churchyard. Often of a night would I steal from between the sheets, and climbing upon the high oak chest that stood before my bedroom window, sit peering down fearfully upon the aged gray tombstones far below, wondering whether the shadows that crept among them might not be ghosts – soiled ghosts that had lost their natural whiteness by long exposure to the city's smoke, and had grown dingy, like the snow that sometimes lay there.

I persuaded myself that they were ghosts, and came, at length, to have quite a friendly feeling for them. I wondered what they thought when they saw the fading letters of their own names upon the stones, whether they remembered themselves and wished they were alive again, or whether they were happier as they were. But that seemed a still sadder idea.

One night, as I sat there watching, I felt a hand upon my shoulder. I was not frightened, because it was a soft, gentle hand that I well knew, so I merely laid my cheek against it.

'What's mumma's naughty boy doing out of bed? Shall I beat him?' And the other hand was laid against my other cheek, and I could feel the soft curls mingling with my own.

'Only looking at the ghosts, ma,' I answered. 'There's such a lot of 'em down there.' Then I added, musingly, 'I wonder what it feels like to be a ghost.'

My mother said nothing, but took me up in her arms, and carried me back to bed, and then, sitting down beside me, and holding my hand in hers – there was not so very much difference in the size – began to sing in that low, caressing voice of hers that always made me feel, for the time being, that I wanted to be a good boy, a song she often used to sing to me, and that I have never heard any one else sing since, and should not care to.

But while she sang, something fell on my hand that caused me to sit up and insist on examining her eyes. She laughed; rather a strange, broken little laugh, I thought, and said it was nothing, and told me to lie still and go to sleep. So I wriggled down again and shut my eyes tight, but I could not understand what had made her cry.

Poor little mother, she had a notion, founded evidently upon inborn belief rather than upon observation, that all children were angels, and that, in consequence, an altogether exceptional demand existed for them in a certain other place, where there are more openings for angels, rendering their retention in this world difficult and undependable. My talk about ghosts must have made that foolishly fond heart ache with a vague dread that night, and for many a night onward, I fear.

For some time after this I would often look up to find my mother's eyes fixed upon me. Especially closely did she watch me at feeding times, and on these occasions, as the meal progressed, her face would acquire an expression of satisfaction and relief.

Once, during dinner, I heard her whisper to my father (for children are not quite so deaf as their elders think), 'He seems to eat all right.'

'Eat!' replied my father in the same penetrating undertone; 'if he dies of anything, it will be of eating.'

So my little mother grew less troubled, and, as the days went by, saw reason to think that my brother angels might consent to do without me for yet a while longer; and I, putting away the child with his ghostly fancies, became, in course of time, a grown-up person, and ceased to believe in ghosts, together with many other things that, perhaps, it were better for a man if he did believe in.

But the memory of that dingy graveyard, and of the shadows that dwelt therein, came back to me very vividly the other day, for it seemed to me as though I were a ghost myself, gliding through the silent streets where once I had passed swiftly, full of life.

Diving into a long unopened drawer, I had, by chance, drawn forth a dusty volume of manuscript, labelled upon its torn brown paper cover, NOVEL NOTES. The scent of dead days clung to its dogs'-eared pages; and, as it lay open before me, my memory wandered back to the summer evenings – not so very long ago, perhaps, if one but adds up the years, but a long, long while ago if one measures Time by feeling – when four friends had sat together making it, who would never sit together any more. With each crumpled leaf I turned, the uncomfortable conviction that I was only a ghost, grew stronger. The handwriting was my own, but the words were the words of a stranger, so that as I read I wondered to myself, saying: did I ever think this? did I really hope that? did I plan to do this? did I resolve to be such? does life, then, look so to the eyes of a young man? not knowing whether to smile or sigh.

The book was a compilation, half diary, half memoranda. In

it lay the record of many musings, of many talks, and out of it – selecting what seemed suitable, adding, altering, and arranging – I have shaped the chapters that hereafter follow.

That I have a right to do so I have fully satisfied my own conscience, an exceptionally fussy one. Of the four joint authors, he whom I call 'MacShaughnassy' has laid aside his title to all things beyond six feet of sun-scorched ground in the African veldt; while from him I have designated 'Brown' I have borrowed but little, and that little I may fairly claim to have made my own by reason of the artistic merit with which I have embellished it. Indeed, in thus taking a few of his bald ideas and shaping them into readable form, am I not doing him a kindness, and thereby returning good for evil? For has he not, slipping from the high ambition of his youth, sunk ever downward step by step, until he has become a critic, and, therefore, my natural enemy? Does he not, in the columns of a certain journal of large pretension but small circulation, call me ''Arry' (without an 'H', the satirical rogue), and is not his contempt for the English-speaking people based chiefly upon the fact that some of them read my books? But in the days of Bloomsbury lodgings and first-night pits we thought each other clever.

From 'Jephson' I hold a letter, dated from a station deep in the heart of the Queensland bush. *'Do what you like with it, dear boy,'* the letter runs, *'so long as you keep me out of it. Thanks for your complimentary regrets, but I cannot share them. I was never fitted for a literary career. Lucky for me, I found it out in time. Some poor devils don't. (I'm not getting at you, old man. We read all your stuff, and like it very much. Time hangs a bit heavy, you know, here, in the winter, and we are glad of almost anything.) This life suits me better. I love to feel my horse between my thighs, and the sun upon my skin. And there are the youngsters growing up about us, and the hands to look after, and the stock. I daresay it seems a very commonplace unintellectual life to you, but it satisfies my nature more than the writing of books could ever do. Besides, there are too many authors as it is. The world is so busy reading and writing, it has no time left for thinking. You'll tell me, of course, that books are thought, but that is only the jargon of the Press. You come out here, old man, and sit as I do sometimes for days and nights together alone with the dumb cattle on an upheaved island of earth, as it were, jutting out into the deep sky, and you will know that they are not. What a man thinks – really thinks – goes down into him and grows in silence. What a man writes in books are the thoughts that he wishes to be thought to think.'*

Poor Jephson! he promised so well at one time. But he always had strange notions.

JJK

CHAPTER I

When, on returning home one evening, after a pipe party at my friend Jephson's, I informed my wife that I was going to write a novel, she expressed herself as pleased with the idea. She said she had often wondered I had never thought of doing so before. 'Look,' she added, 'how silly all the novels are nowadays; I'm sure you could write one.' (Ethelbertha intended to be complimentary, I am convinced; but there is a looseness about her mode of expression which, at times, renders her meaning obscure.)

When, however, I told her that my friend Jephson was going to collaborate with me, she remarked, 'Oh,' in a doubtful tone; and when I further went on to explain to her that Selkirk Brown and Derrick MacShaughnassy were also going to assist, she replied, 'Oh,' in a tone which contained no trace of doubtfulness whatever, and from which it was clear that her interest in the matter, as a practical scheme, had entirely evaporated.

I fancy that the fact of my three collaborators being all bachelors diminished somewhat our chances of success, in Ethelbertha's mind. Against bachelors, as a class, she entertains a strong prejudice. A man's not having sense enough to want to marry, or, having that, not having wit enough to do it, argues to her thinking either weakness of intellect or natural depravity, the former rendering its victim unable, and the latter unfit, ever to become a really useful novelist.

I tried to make her understand the peculiar advantages our plan possessed.

'You see,' I explained, 'in the usual common-place novel we

'I'm sure you could write one'

only get, as a matter of fact, one person's ideas. Now, in this novel, there will be four clever men all working together. The public will thus be enabled to obtain the thoughts and opinions of the whole four of us, at the price usually asked for merely one author's views. If the British reader knows his own business, he will order this book early, to avoid disappointment. Such an opportunity may not occur again for years.'

Ethelbertha agreed that this was probable.

'Besides,' I continued, my enthusiasm waxing stronger the more I reflected upon the matter, 'this work is going to be a genuine bargain in another way also. We are not going to put our mere everyday ideas into it. We are going to crowd into this one novel all the wit and wisdom that the whole four of us possess, if the book will hold it. We shall not write another novel after this one. Indeed, we shall not be able to; we shall have nothing more to write. This work will partake of the nature of an intellectual clearance sale. We are going to put into this novel simply all we know.'

Ethelbertha shut her lips, and said something inside; and then remarked aloud that she supposed it would be a one volume affair.

I felt hurt at the implied sneer. I pointed out to her that there already existed a numerous body of specially-trained men employed to do nothing else but make disagreeable observations upon authors and their works — a duty that, so far as I could judge, they seemed capable of performing without any amateur assistance whatever. And I hinted that, by his own fireside, a literary man looked to breathe a more sympathetic atmosphere.

Ethelbertha replied that of course I knew what she meant. She said that she was not thinking of me, and that Jephson was, no doubt, sensible enough (Jephson is engaged), but she did not see the object of bringing half the parish into it. (Nobody suggested bringing 'half the parish' into it. Ethelbertha will talk so wildly.) To suppose that Brown and MacShaughnassy could be of any use whatever, she considered absurd. What could a couple of raw bachelors know about life and human nature? As regarded MacShaughnassy in particular, she was of opinion that if we only wanted out of him all that *he* knew, and could keep him to the subject, we ought to be able to get that into about a page.

My wife's present estimate of MacShaughnassy's knowledge is the result of reaction. The first time she ever saw him, she and he got on wonderfully well together; and when I returned to the drawing-room, after seeing him down to the gate, her first words were, 'What a wonderful man that Mr MacShaughnassy is. He seems to know so much about everything.'

That describes MacShaughnassy exactly. He does seem to know a tremendous lot. He is possessed of more information than any man I ever came across. Occasionally, it is correct information; but, speaking broadly, it is remarkable for its marvellous unreliability. Where he gets it from is a secret that nobody has ever yet been able to fathom.

Ethelbertha was very young when we started housekeeping. (Our first butcher very nearly lost her custom, I remember, once and for ever by calling her 'Missie,' and giving her a message to take back to her mother. She arrived home in tears. She said that perhaps she wasn't fit to be anybody's wife, but she did not see why she should be told so by the tradespeople.) She was naturally somewhat inexperienced in domestic affairs, and, feeling this keenly, was grateful to any one who would give her useful hints and advice. When MacShaughnassy came along he seemed, in her eyes, a sort of glorified Mrs Beeton. He knew everything wanted to be known inside a house, from the scientific method of peeling a potato to the cure of spasms in cats, and Ethelbertha would sit at his feet, figuratively speaking, and gain enough information in one evening to make the house unlivable in for a month.

He told her how fires ought to be laid. He said that the way fires were usually laid in this country was contrary to all the laws of nature, and he showed her how the thing was done in Crim Tartary, or some such place, where the science of laying fires is alone properly understood. He proved to her that an immense saving in time and labour, to say nothing of coals, could be effected by the adoption of the Crim Tartary system; and he taught it to her then and there, and she went straight downstairs and explained it to the girl.

Amenda, our then 'general,' was an extremely stolid young

person, and, in some respects, a model servant. She never argued. She never seemed to have any notions of her own whatever. She accepted our ideas without comment, and carried them out with such pedantic precision and such evident absence of all feeling of responsibility concerning the result as to surround our home legislation with quite a military atmosphere.

On the present occasion she stood quietly by while the MacShaughnassy method of fire-laying was expounded to her. When Ethelbertha had finished she simply said:–

'You want me to lay the fires like that?'

'Yes, Amenda, we'll always have the fires laid like that in future, if you please.'

'All right, mum,' replied Amenda, with perfect unconcern, and there the matter ended, for that evening.

On coming downstairs the next morning we found the breakfast table

But there was no breakfast

spread very nicely, but there was no breakfast. We waited. Ten minutes went by – a quarter of an hour – twenty minutes. Then Ethelbertha rang the bell. In response Amenda presented, herself, calm and respectful.

'Do you know that the proper time for breakfast is half-past eight, Amenda?'

'Yes'm.'

'And do you know that it's now nearly nine?'

'Yes'm.'

'Well, isn't breakfast ready?'

'No, mum.'

'Will it *ever* be ready?'

'Well, mum,' replied Amenda, in a tone of genial frankness, 'to tell you the truth, I don't think it ever will.'

'What's the reason? Won't the fire light?'

'Oh yes, it lights all right.'

'Well, then, why can't you cook the breakfast?'

'Because before you can turn yourself round it goes out again.'

Amenda never volunteered statements. She answered the question put to her and then stopped dead. I called downstairs to her on one occasion, before I understood her peculiarities, to ask her if she knew the time. She replied, 'Yes, sir,' and disappeared into the back kitchen. At the end of thirty seconds or so, I called down again. 'I asked you, Amenda,' I said reproachfully, 'to tell me the time about ten minutes ago.'

'Oh, did you?' she called back pleasantly. 'I beg your pardon. I thought you asked me if I knew it – it's half-past four.'

Ethelbertha inquired – to return to our fire – if she had tried lighting it again.

'Oh yes, mum,' answered the girl. 'I've tried four times.' Then she added cheerfully, 'I'll try again if you like, mum.'

Amenda was the most willing servant we ever paid wages to.

Ethelbertha said she would step down and light the fire herself, and told Amenda to follow her and watch how she did it. I felt interested in the experiment, and followed also. Ethelbertha tucked up her frock and set to work. Amenda and I stood around and looked on.

At the end of half an hour Ethelbertha retired from the contest, hot, dirty, and a trifle irritable. The fireplace retained the same cold, cynical expression with which it had greeted our entrance.

Then I tried. I honestly tried my best. I was eager and anxious to succeed. For one reason, I wanted my breakfast. For another, I wanted to be able to say that I had done this thing. It seemed to me that for any human being to light a fire, laid as that fire was laid, would be a feat to be proud of. To light a fire even under ordinary circumstances is not too easy a task: to do so, handicapped by MacShaughnassy's rules, would, I felt, be an achievement pleasant to look back upon. My idea, had I succeeded, would have been to go round the neighbourhood and brag about it.

However, I did not succeed. I lit various other things, including the kitchen carpet and the cat, who would come sniffing about, but the materials within the stove appeared to be fire-proof.

Ethelbertha and I sat down, one each side of our cheerless hearth, and looked at one another, and thought of MacShaughnassy, until Amenda chimed in on our despair with one of those practical suggestions of hers that she occasionally threw out for us to accept or not, as we chose.

'Maybe,' said she, 'I'd better light it in the old way just for to-day.'

'Do, Amenda,' said Ethelbertha, rising. And then she added, 'I think we'll always have them lighted in the old way, Amenda, if you please.'

Another time he showed us how to make coffee – according to the Arabian method. Arabia must be a very untidy country if they make coffee often over there. He dirtied two saucepans, three jugs, one tablecloth, one nutmeg-grater, one hearthrug, three cups, and himself. This made coffee for two – what would have been necessary in the case of a party, one dares not think.

That we did not like the coffee when made, MacShaughnassy attributed to our debased taste – the result of long indulgence in an inferior article. He drank both cups himself, and afterwards went home in a cab.

He had an aunt in those days, I remember, a mysterious old lady, who lived in some secluded retreat from where she wrought incalculable mischief upon MacShaughnassy's friends. What he did not know – the one or two things that he was *not* an authority upon – this aunt of his knew. 'No,' he would say with engaging candour – 'no, that is a thing I cannot advise you about myself. But,' he would add, 'I'll tell you what I'll do. I'll write to my aunt and ask her.' And a day or two afterwards he would call again, bringing his aunt's advice with him; and, if you were young and inexperienced, or a natural born fool, you might possibly follow it.

She sent us a recipe on one occasion, through MacShaughnassy, for the extermination of blackbeetles. We occupied a very picturesque old house; but, as with most picturesque old houses, its advantages were chiefly external. There were many holes and cracks and crevices within its creaking framework. Frogs, who had lost their way and taken the wrong turning, would suddenly discover themselves in the middle of our dining-room, apparently quite as much to their own surprise and annoyance as to ours. A numerous company of rats and mice, remarkably fond of physical exercise, had fitted the place up as a gymnasium for themselves; and our kitchen, after ten o'clock, was turned into a blackbeetles' club. They came up through the floor and out through the walls, and gambolled there in their light-hearted, reckless way till daylight.

The rats and mice Amenda did not object to. She said she liked to watch them. But against the blackbeetles she was prejudiced. Therefore, when my wife informed her that MacShaughnassy's aunt had given us an infallible recipe for their annihilation, she rejoiced.

We purchased the materials, manufactured the mixture, and put it about. The beetles came and ate it. They seemed to like it. They finished it all up, and were evidently vexed that there was not more. But they did not die.

We told these facts to MacShaughnassy. He smiled, a very

grim smile, and said in a low tone, full of meaning, 'Let them eat!'

It appeared that this was one of those slow, insidious poisons. It did not kill the beetle off immediately, but it undermined his constitution. Day by day he would sink and droop without being able to tell what was the matter with himself, until one morning we should enter the kitchen to find him lying cold and very still.

So we made more stuff and laid it round each night, and the blackbeetles from all about the parish swarmed to it. Each night they came in greater quantities. They fetched up all their friends and relations. Strange beetles – beetles from other families, with no claim on us whatever – got to hear about the thing, and came in hordes, and tried to rob our blackbeetles of it. By the end of a week we had lured into our kitchen every beetle that wasn't lame for miles round.

MacShaughnassy said it was a good thing. We should clear the suburb at one swoop. The beetles had now been eating this poison steadily for ten days, and he said that the end could not be far off. I was glad to hear it, because I was beginning to find this unlimited hospitality expensive. It was a dear poison that we were giving them, and they were hearty eaters.

We went downstairs to see how they were getting on. MacShaughnassy thought they seemed queer, and was of opinion that they were breaking up. Speaking for myself, I can only say that a healthier-looking lot of beetles I never wish to see.

One, it is true, did die that very evening. He was detected in the act of trying to make off with an unfairly large portion of the poison, and three or four of the others set upon him savagely and killed him.

But he was the only one, so far as I could ever discover, to whom MacShaughnassy's recipe proved fatal. As for the others, they grew fat and sleek upon it. Some of them, indeed, began to acquire quite a figure. We lessened their numbers

eventually by the help of some common oil-shop stuff. But
such vast numbers, attracted by MacShaughnassy's poison,
had settled in the house, that to finally exterminate them now
was hopeless.

I have not heard of MacShaughnassy's aunt lately. Possibly,
one of MacShaughnassy's bosom friends has found out her
address and has gone down and murdered her. If so, I should
like to thank him.

I tried a little while ago to cure MacShaughnassy of his fatal
passion for advice-giving, by repeating to him a very sad story
that was told to me by a gentleman I met in an American
railway car. I was travelling from Buffalo to New York, and,
during the day, it suddenly occurred to me that I might make
the journey more interesting by leaving the cars at Albany and
completing the distance by water. But I did not know how the
boats ran, and I had no guide-book with me. I glanced about
for some one to question. A mild-looking, elderly gentleman
sat by the next window reading a book, the cover of which was
familiar to me. I deemed him to be intelligent, and approached
him.

'I beg your pardon for interrupting you,' I said, sitting down
opposite to him, 'but could you give me any information about
the boats between Albany and New York?'

'Well,' he answered, looking up with a pleasant smile, 'there
are three lines of boats altogether. There is the Heggarty line,
but they only go as far as Catskill. Then there are the
Poughkeepsie boats, which go every other day. Or there is
what we call the canal boat.'

'Oh,' I said. 'Well now, which would you advise me to ——'

He jumped to his feet with a cry, and stood glaring down at
me with a gleam in his eyes which was positively murderous.

'You villain!' he hissed in low tones of concentrated fury, 'so
that's your game, is it? I'll give you something that you'll want
advice about,' and he whipped out a six-chambered revolver.

I felt hurt. I also felt that if the interview were prolonged I might feel even more hurt. So I left him without a word, and drifted over to the other end of the car, where I took up a position between a stout lady and the door.

I was still musing upon the incident, when, looking up, I observed my elderly friend making towards me. I rose and laid my hand upon the door-knob. He should not find me unprepared. He smiled, reassuringly, however, and held out his hand.

'I've been thinking,' he said, 'that maybe I was a little rude just now. I should like, if you will let me, to explain. I think, when you have heard my story, you will understand, and forgive me.'

There was that about him which made me trust him. We found a quiet corner in the smoking-car. I had a 'whiskey sour', and he prescribed for himself a strange thing of his own invention. Then we lighted our cigars, and he talked.

'Thirty years ago,' said he, 'I was a young man with a healthy belief in myself, and a desire to do good to others. I did not imagine myself a genius. I did not even consider myself exceptionally brilliant or talented. But it did seem to me, and the more I noted the doings of my fellow-men and women, the more assured did I become of it, that I possessed plain, practical common sense to an unusual and remarkable degree. Conscious of this, I wrote a little book, which I entitled *How to be Happy, Wealthy, and Wise*, and published it at my own expense. I did not seek for profit. I merely wished to be useful.

'The book did not make the stir that I had anticipated. Some two or three hundred copies went off, and then the sale practically ceased.

'I confess that at first I was disappointed. But after a while, I reflected that, if people would not take my advice, it was more their loss than mine, and I dismissed that matter from my mind.

'One morning, about a twelvemonth afterwards, I was sitting in my study, when the servant entered to say that there was a man downstairs who wanted very much to see me.

'I gave instructions that he should be sent up, and up accordingly he came.

'He was a common man, but he had an open, intelligent countenance, and his manner was most respectful. I motioned him to be seated. He selected a chair, and sat down on the extreme edge of it.

'"I hope you'll pard'n this intrusion, sir," he began, speaking deliberately, and twirling his hat the while; "but I've come more'n two hundred miles to see you, sir."

'I expressed myself as pleased, and he continued: "They tell me, sir, as you're the gentleman as wrote that little book, *How to be Happy, Wealthy, and Wise.*" He enumerated the three items slowly, dwelling lovingly on each. I admitted the fact.

'"Ah, that's a wonderful book, sir," he went on. "I ain't one of them as has got brains of their own – not to speak of – but I know enough to know them as has; and when I read that little book, I says to myself, Josiah Hackett (that's my name, sir), when you're in doubt

'A common man, but he had an open, intelligent countenance'

don't you get addling that thick head o' yours, as will only tell you all wrong; you go to the gentleman as wrote that little book and ask him for his advice. He is a kind-hearted gentleman, as any one can tell, and he'll give it you; and *when* you've got it, you go straight ahead, full steam, and don't you stop for nothing, 'cause he'll know what's best for you, same as he knows what's best for everybody. That's what I says, sir; and that's what I'm here for."

'He paused, and wiped his brow with a green cotton handkerchief. I prayed him to proceed.

'It appeared that the worthy fellow wanted to marry, but could not make up his mind *whom* he wanted to marry. He had his eye – so he expressed it – upon two young women, and they, he had reason to believe, regarded him in return with more than usual favour. His difficulty was to decide which of the two – both of them excellent and deserving young persons – would make him the best wife. The one, Juliana, the only daughter of a retired sea-captain, he described as a winsome lassie. The other, Hannah, was an older and altogether more womanly girl. She was the eldest of a large family. Her father, he said, was a God-fearing man, and was doing well in the timber trade. He asked me which of them I should advise him to marry.

'I was flattered. What man in my position would not have been? This Josiah Hackett had come from afar to hear my wisdom. He was willing – nay, anxious – to entrust his whole life's happiness to my discretion. That he was wise in so doing, I entertained no doubt. The choice of a wife I had always held to be a matter needing a calm, unbiassed judgment, such as no lover could possibly bring to bear upon the subject. In such a case, I should not have hesitated to offer advice to the wisest of men. To this poor, simple-minded fellow, I felt it would be cruel to refuse it.

'He handed me photographs of both the young persons under consideration. I jotted down on the back of each such particulars as I deemed would assist me in estimating their respective fitness for the vacancy in question, and promised to carefully consider the problem, and write him in a day or two.

'His gratitude was touching. "Don't you trouble to write no letters, sir," he said; "you just stick down 'Julia' or 'Hannah' on a bit of paper, and put it in an envelope. I shall know what it means, and that's the one as I shall marry."

'Then he gripped me by the hand and left me.

'I gave a good deal of thought to the selection of Josiah's wife. I wanted him to be happy.

'Juliana was certainly very pretty. There was a lurking playfulness about the corners of Juliana's mouth which conjured up the sound of rippling laughter. Had I acted on impulse, I should have clasped Juliana in Josiah's arms.

'But, I reflected, more sterling qualities than mere playfulness and prettiness are needed for a wife. Hannah, though not so charming, clearly possessed both energy and sense – qualities highly necessary to a poor man's wife. Hannah's father was a pious man, and was "doing well" – a thrifty, saving man, no doubt. He would have instilled into her lessons of economy and virtue; and, later on, she might possibly come in for a little something. She was the eldest of a large family. She was sure to have had to help her mother a good deal. She would be experienced in household matters, and would understand the bringing up of children.

'Julia's father, on the other hand, was a retired sea-captain. Seafaring folk are generally loose sort of fish. He had probably been in the habit of going about the house, using language and expressing views, the hearing of which could not but have exercised an injurious effect upon the formation of a growing girl's character. Juliana was his only child. Only children generally make bad men and women. They are allowed to have their own way too much. The pretty daughter of a retired sea-captain would be certain to be spoilt.

'Josiah, I had also to remember, was a man evidently of weak character. He would need management. Now, there was something about Hannah's eye that eminently suggested management.

'At the end of two days my mind was made up. I wrote "Hannah" on a slip of paper, and posted it.

'A fortnight afterwards I received a letter from Josiah. He thanked me for my advice, but added, incidentally, that he wished I could have made it Julia. However, he said, he felt sure I knew best, and by the time I received the letter he and Hannah would be one.

'That letter worried me. I began to wonder if, after all, I had chosen the right girl. Suppose Hannah was not all I thought her! What a terrible thing it would be for Josiah. What data, sufficient to reason upon, had I possessed? How did I know that Hannah was not a lazy, ill-tempered girl, a continual thorn in the side of her poor, overworked mother, and a perpetual blister to her younger brothers and sisters? How did I know she had been well brought up? Her father might be a precious old fraud: most seemingly pious men are. She may have learned from him only hypocrisy.

'Then also, how did I know that Juliana's merry childishness would not ripen into sweet, cheerful womanliness? Her father, for all I knew to the contrary, might be the model of what a retired sea-captain should be; with possibly a snug little sum safely invested somewhere. And Juliana was his only child. What reason had I for rejecting this fair young creature's love for Josiah?

'I took her photo from my desk. I seemed to detect a reproachful look in the big eyes. I saw before me the scene in the little far-away home when the first tidings of Josiah's marriage fell like a cruel stone into the hitherto placid waters of her life. I saw her kneeling by her father's chair, while the white-haired, bronzed old man gently stroked the golden head, shaking with silent sobs against his breast. My remorse was almost more than I could bear.

'I put her aside and took up Hannah – my chosen one. She seemed to be regarding me with a smile of heartless triumph. There began to take possession of me a feeling of positive dislike to Hannah.

'I fought against the feeling. I told myself it was prejudice. But the more I reasoned against it the stronger it became. I could tell that, as the days went by, it would grow from dislike to loathing, from loathing to hate. And this was the woman I had deliberately selected as a life companion for Josiah!

'For weeks I knew no peace of mind. Every letter that arrived I dreaded to open, fearing it might be from Josiah. At every knock I started up, and looked about for a hiding-place. Every time I came across the heading, "Domestic Tragedy," in the newspapers, I broke into a cold perspiration. I expected to read that Josiah and Hannah had murdered each other, and died cursing me.

'As the time went by, however, and I heard nothing, my fears began to assuage, and my belief in my own intuitive good judgment to return. Maybe, I had done a good thing for Josiah and Hannah, and they were blessing me. Three years passed peacefully away, and I was beginning to forget the existence of the Hacketts.

'Then he came again. I returned home from business one evening to find him waiting for me in the hall. The moment I saw him I knew that my worst fears had fallen short of the truth. I motioned him to follow me to my study. He did so, and seated himself in the identical chair on which he had sat three years ago. The change in him was remarkable; he looked old and careworn. His manner was that of resigned hopelessness.

'We remained for a while without speaking, he twirling his hat as at our first interview, I making a show of arranging papers on my desk. At length, feeling that anything would be more bearable than this silence, I turned to him.

'"Things have not been going well with you, I'm afraid, Josiah?" I said.

'"No, sir," he replied quietly: "I can't say as they have, altogether. That Hannah of yours has turned out a bit of a teaser."

'There was no touch of reproach in his tones. He simply stated a melancholy fact.

'"But she is a good wife to you in other ways," I urged. "She has her faults, of course. We all have. But she is energetic. Come now, you will admit she's energetic."

'I owed it to myself to find some good in Hannah, and this was the only thing I could think of at that moment.

'"Oh yes, she's that," he assented. "A little too much so for our sized house, I sometimes think."

'"You see," he went on, "she's a bit cornery in her temper, Hannah is; and then her mother's a bit trying, at times."

'They ain't scattered much'

'"Her mother!" I exclaimed, "but what's *she* got to do with you?"

'"Well, you see, sir," he answered, "she's living with us now – ever since the old man went off."

'"Hannah's father! Is he dead, then?"

'"Well, not exactly, sir," he replied. "He ran off about a twelvemonth ago with one of the young women who used to teach in the Sunday School, and joined the Mormons. It came as a great surprise to every one."

'I groaned. "And his business," I inquired – "the timber business, who carries that on?"

'"Oh, that!" answered Josiah. "Oh, that had to be sold to pay his debts – leastways, to go towards 'em."

'I remarked what a terrible thing it was for his family. I supposed the home was broken up, and they were all scattered.

'"No, sir," he replied simply, "they ain't scattered much. They're all living with us."

'"But there," he continued, seeing the look upon my face; "of course, all this has nothing to do with you, sir. You've got troubles of your own, I daresay, sir. I didn't come here to worry you with mine. That would be a poor return for all your kindness to me."

'"What has become of Julia?" I asked. I did not feel I wanted to question him any more about his own affairs.

'A smile broke the settled melancholy of his features. "Ah," he said, in a more cheerful tone than he had hitherto employed, "it does one good to think about *her*, it does. She's married to a friend of mine now, young Sam Jessop. I slips out and gives 'em a call now and then, when Hannah ain't round. Lord, it's like getting a glimpse of heaven to look into their little home. He often chaffs me about it, Sam does. 'Well, you *was* a sawny-headed chunk, Josiah, *you* was,' he often says to me. We're old chums, you know, sir, Sam and me, so he don't mind joking a bit like."

'Then the smile died away, and he added with a sigh, "Yes, I've often thought since, sir, how jolly it would have been if you could have seen your way to making it Juliana."

'I felt I must get him back to Hannah at any cost. I said, "I suppose you and you wife are still living in the old place?"

'"Yes," he replied, "if you can call it living. It's a hard struggle with so many of us."

'He said he did not know how he should have managed if it had not been for the help of Julia's father. He said the captain had behaved more like an angel than anything else he knew of.

'"I don't say as he's one of your clever sort, you know, sir," he explained. "Not the man as one would go to for advice, like one would to you, sir; but he's a good sort for all that."

'"And that reminds me, sir," he went on, "of what I've come here about. You'll think it very bold of me to ask, sir, but ——"

'I interrupted him. "Josiah," I said, "I admit that I am much to blame for what has come upon you. You asked me for my advice, and I gave it you. Which of us was the bigger idiot, we will not discuss. The point is that I did give it, and I am not a man to shirk my responsibilities. What, in reason, you ask, and I can grant, I will give you."

'He was overcome with gratitude. "I knew it, sir," he said. "I knew you would not refuse me. I said so to Hannah. I said, 'I will go to that gentleman and ask him. I will go to him and ask him for his advice.'"

'I said: "His what?"

'"His advice," repeated Josiah, apparently surprised at my tone, "on a little matter as I can't quite make up my mind about."

'I thought at first he was trying to be sarcastic, but he wasn't. That man sat there, and wrestled with me for my advice as to whether he should invest a thousand dollars which Julia's father had offered to lend him, in the purchase of a laundry business or a bar. He hadn't had enough of it (my advice, I mean); he wanted it again, and he spun me reasons why I should give it him. The choice of a wife was a different thing altogether, he argued. Perhaps he ought *not* to have asked me for my opinion as to that. But advice as to which of two trades a man would do best to select, surely any business man could give. He said he had just been reading again my little book, *How to be Happy*, etc., and if the gentleman who wrote that could not decide between the respective merits of one particular laundry and one particular bar, both situate in the same city, well, then, all he had got to say was that knowledge and wisdom were clearly of no practical use in this world whatever.

'Well, it did seem a simple thing to advise a man about. Surely as to a matter of this kind, I, a professed business man, must be able to form a sounder judgment than this poor pumpkin-headed lamb. It would be heartless to refuse to help him. I promised to look into the matter, and let him know what I thought.

'He rose and shook me by the hand. He said he would not try to thank me; words would only seem weak. He dashed away a tear and went out.

'I brought an amount of thought to bear upon this thousand-dollar investment sufficient to have floated a bank. I did not mean to make another Hannah job, if I could help it. I studied the papers Josiah had left with me, but did not attempt to form any opinion from them. I went down quietly to Josiah's city, and inspected both businesses on the spot. I instituted secret but searching inquiries in the neighbourhood. I disguised myself as a simple-minded

'I disguised myself as a simple-minded young man'

young man who had come into a little money, and wormed myself into the confidence of the servants. I interviewed half the town upon the pretence that I was writing the commercial history of New England, and should like some particulars of their career, and I invariably ended my examination by asking them which was their favourite bar, and where they got their washing done. I stayed a fortnight in the town. Most of my spare time I spent at the bar. In my leisure moments I dirtied my clothes so that they might be washed at the laundry.

'As the result of my investigations I discovered that, so far as the two businesses themselves were concerned, there was not a pin to choose between them. It became merely a question of which particular trade would best suit the Hacketts.

'I reflected. The keeper of a bar was exposed to much temptation. A weak-minded man, mingling continually in the company of topers, might possibly end by giving way to drink. Now, Josiah was an exceptionally weak-minded man. It had also to be borne in mind that he had a shrewish wife, and that her whole family had come to live with him. Clearly, to place Josiah in a position of easy access to unlimited liquor would be madness.

'About a laundry, on the other hand, there was something soothing. The working of a laundry needed many hands. Hannah's relatives might be used up in a laundry, and made to earn their own living. Hannah might expend her energy in flat-ironing, and Josiah could turn the mangle. The idea conjured up quite a pleasant domestic picture. I recommended the laundry.

'On the following Monday, Josiah wrote to say that he had bought the laundry. On Tuesday I read in the *Commercial Intelligence* that one of the most remarkable features of the time was the marvellous rise taking place all over New England in the value of hotel and bar property. On Thursday, in the list of failures, I came across no less than four laundry proprietors; and the paper added, in explanation, that the American washing industry, owing to the rapid growth of Chinese competition, was practically on its last legs. I went out and got drunk.

'My life became a curse to me. All day long I thought of Josiah. All night I dreamed of him. Suppose that, not content with being the cause of his domestic misery, I had now deprived him of the means of earning a livelihood, and had rendered useless the generosity of that good old sea-captain. I began to appear to myself as a malignant fiend, ever following this simple but worthy man to work evil upon him.

'Time passed away, however; I heard nothing from or of him, and my burden at last fell from me.

'Then at the end of about five years he came again.

'He came behind me as I was opening the door with my latch-key, and laid an unsteady hand upon my arm. It was a dark night, but a gas-lamp showed me his face. I recognised it in spite of the red blotches and the bleary film that hid the eyes. I caught him roughly by the arm, and hurried him inside and up into my study.

'"Sit down," I hissed, "and tell me the worst first."

'He was about to select his favourite chair. I felt that if I saw him and that particular chair in association for the third time, I should do something terrible to both. I snatched it away from him, and he sat down heavily on the floor, and burst into tears. I let him remain there, and, thickly, between hiccoughs, he told his tale.

'The laundry had gone from bad to worse. A new railway had come to the town, altering its whole topography. The business and residential portion had gradually shifted north- ward. The spot where the bar – the particular one which I had rejected for the laundry – had formerly stood was now the commercial centre of the city. The man who had purchased it in place of Josiah had sold out and made a fortune. The southern area (where the laundry was situate) was, it had been discovered, built upon a swamp, and was in a highly unsanitary condition. Careful housewives naturally objected to sending their washing into such a neighbourhood.

'Other troubles had also come. The baby – Josiah's pet, the one bright thing in life – had fallen into the copper and been boiled. Hannah's mother had been crushed in the mangle, and was now a helpless cripple, who had to be waited on day and night.

'Under these accumulated misfortunes Josiah had sought consolation in drink, and had become a hopeless sot. He felt his degradation keenly, and wept copiously. He said he thought that in a cheerful place, such as a bar, he might have been strong and brave; but that there was something about the everlasting smell of damp clothes and suds, that seemed to sap his manhood.

'I asked him what the captain had said to it all. He burst into fresh tears, and replied that the captain was no more. That, he added, reminded him of what he had come about. The good-hearted old fellow had bequeathed him five thousand dollars. He wanted my advice as to how to invest it.

'My first impulse was to kill him on the spot. I wish now that I had. I restrained myself, however, and offered him the alternative of being thrown from the window or of leaving by the door without another word.

'He answered that he was quite prepared to go by the window if I would first tell him whether to put his money in the Terra del Fuego Nitrate Company, Limited, or in the Union Pacific Bank. Life had no further interest for him. All he cared for was to feel that this little nest-egg was safely laid by for the benefit of his beloved ones after he was gone.

'He pressed me to tell him what I thought of nitrates. I replied that I declined to say anything whatever on the subject. He assumed from my answer that I did not think much of nitrates, and announced his intention of investing the money, in consequence, in the Union Pacific Bank.

'I told him by all means to do so, if he liked.

'He paused, and seemed to be puzzling it out. Then he smiled knowingly, and said he thought he understood what I meant. It was very kind of me. He should put every dollar he possessed in the Terra del Fuego Nitrate Company.

'He rose (with difficulty) to go. I stopped him. I knew, as certainly as I knew the sun would rise the next morning, that whichever company I advised him, or he persisted in thinking I had advised him (which was the same thing), to invest in, would, sooner or later, come to smash. My grandmother had all her little fortune in the Terra del Fuego Nitrate Company. I could not see her brought to penury in her old age. As for Josiah, it could make no difference to him whatever. He would lose his money in any event. I advised him to invest in Union Pacific Bank Shares. He went and did it.

'The Union Pacific Bank held out for eighteen months. Then it began to totter. The financial world stood bewildered. It had always been reckoned one of the safest banks in the country. People asked what could be the cause. I knew well enough, but I did not tell.

'The Bank made a gallant fight, but the hand of fate was upon it. At the end of another nine months the crash came.

'(Nitrates, it need hardly be said, had all this time been going up by leaps and bounds. My grandmother died worth a million dollars, and left the whole of it to a charity. Had she known how I had saved her from ruin, she might have been more grateful.)

'A few days after the failure of the Bank, Josiah arrived on my doorstep; and, this time, he brought his families with him. There were sixteen of them in all.

'What was I to do? I had brought these people step by step to the verge of starvation. I had laid waste alike their happiness and their prospects in life. The least amends I could make was to see that at all events they did not want for the necessities of existence.

'That was seventeen years ago. I am still seeing that they do not want for the necessities of existence; and my conscience is growing easier by noticing that they seem contented with their lot. There are twenty-two of them now, and we have hopes of another in the spring.

'That is my story,' he said. 'Perhaps you will now understand my sudden emotion when you asked for my advice. As a matter of fact, I do not give advice now on any subject.'

I told this tale to MacShaughnassy. He agreed with me that it was instructive, and said he should remember it. He said he should remember it so as to tell it to some fellows that he knew, to whom he thought the lesson should prove useful.

CHAPTER II

I can't honestly say that we made much progress at our first meeting. It was Brown's fault. He would begin by telling us a story about a dog. It was the old, old story of the dog who had been in the habit of going every morning to a certain baker's shop with a penny in his mouth, in exchange for which he always received a penny bun. One day, the baker, thinking he would not know the difference, tried to palm off upon the poor animal a ha'penny bun, whereupon the dog walked straight outside and fetched in a policeman. Brown had heard this chestnut for the first time that afternoon, and was full of it. It is always a mystery to me where Brown has been for the last hundred years. He stops you in the street with, 'Oh, I must tell you! – such a capital story!' And he thereupon proceeds to relate to you, with much spirit and gusto, one of Noah's best known jokes, or some story that Romulus must have originally told to Remus. One of

Some story that Romulus must have originally told to Remus

these days somebody will tell him the history of Adam and Eve, and he will think he has got hold of a new plot, and will work it up into a novel.

He gives forth these hoary antiquities as personal reminiscences of his own, or, at furthest, as episodes in the life of his second cousin. There are certain strange and moving catastrophes that would seem either to have occurred to, or to have been witnessed by, nearly every one you meet. I never came across a man yet who had not seen some other man jerked off the top of an omnibus into a mud-cart. Half London must, at one time or another, have been jerked off omnibuses into mud-carts, and have been fished out at the end of a shovel.

Then there is the tale of the lady whose husband is taken suddenly ill one night at an hotel. She rushes downstairs, and prepares a stiff mustard plaster to put on him, and runs up with it again. In her excitement, however, she charges into the wrong room, and rolling down the bedclothes, presses it lovingly upon the wrong man. I have heard that story so often that I am quite nervous about going to bed in an hotel now. Each man who has told it me has invariably slept in the room next door to that of the victim, and has been awakened by the man's yell as the plaster came down upon him. That is how he (the story-teller) came to know all about it.

Brown wanted us to believe that this prehistoric animal he had been telling us about had belonged to his brother-in-law, and was hurt when Jephson murmured, *sotto voce*, that that made the twenty-eighth man he had met whose brother-in-law had owned that dog – to say nothing of the hundred and seventeen who had owned it themselves.

We tried to get to work afterwards, but Brown had unsettled us for the evening. It is a wicked thing to start dog stories among a party of average sinful men. Let one man tell a dog story, and every other man in the room feels he wants to tell a bigger one.

There is a story going – I cannot vouch for its truth, it was told me by a judge – of a man who lay dying. The pastor of the parish, a good and pious man, came to sit with him, and, thinking to cheer him up, told him an anecdote about a dog. When the pastor had finished, the sick man sat up, and said, 'I know a better story than that. I had a dog once, a big, brown, lop-sided ——'

The effort had proved too much for his strength. He fell back upon the pillows, and the doctor, stepping forward, saw that it was a question only of minutes.

The good old pastor rose, and took the poor fellow's hand in his, and pressed it. 'We shall meet again,' he gently said.

The sick man turned towards him with a consoled and grateful look.

'I'm glad to hear you say that,' he feebly murmured. 'Remind me about that dog.'

Then he passed peacefully away, with a sweet smile upon his pale lips.

Brown, who had had his dog story and was satisfied, wanted us to settle our heroine; but the rest of us did not feel equal to settling any-body just then. We were think-ing of all the true dog stories we had ever heard, and wondering which was the one least likely to be generally disbelieved.

MacShaughnassy, in

Told him an anecdote about a dog

particular, was growing every moment more restless and moody. Brown concluded a long discourse – to which nobody had listened – by remarking with some pride, 'What more can you want? The plot has never been used before, and the characters are entirely original!'

Then MacShaughnassy gave way. 'Talking of plots,' he said, hitching his chair a little nearer the table, 'that puts me in mind. Did I ever tell you about that dog we had when we lived in Norwood?'

'It's not that one about the bull-dog, is it?' queried Jephson anxiously.

'Well, it was a bull-dog,' admitted MacShaughnassy, 'but I don't think I've ever told it you before.'

We knew, by experience, that to argue the matter would only prolong the torture, so we let him go on.

'A great many burglaries had lately taken place in our neighbourhood,' he began, 'and the pater came to the conclusion that it was time he laid down a dog. He thought a bull-dog would be the best for his purpose, and he purchased the most savage and murderous-looking specimen that he could find.

'My mother was alarmed when she saw the dog. "Surely you're not going to let that brute loose about the house" she exclaimed. "He'll kill somebody. I can see it in his face."

'"I want him to kill somebody," replied my father; "I want him to kill burglars."

'"I don't like to hear you talk like that, Thomas," answered the mater; "it's not like you. We've a right to protect our property, but we've no right to take a fellow human creature's life."

'"Our fellow human creatures will be all right so long as they don't come into our kitchen when they've no business there," retorted my father, somewhat testily. "I'm going to fix up this dog in the scullery, and if a burglar comes fooling around – well that's *his* affair."

'The old folks quarrelled on and off for about a month over

this dog. The dad thought the mater absurdly sentimental, and the mater thought the dad unnecessarily vindictive. Meanwhile the dog grew more ferocious-looking every day.

'One night my mother woke my father up with: "Thomas,

'Thomas, there's a burglar downstairs'

there's a burglar downstairs, I'm positive. I distinctly heard the kitchen door open."

'"Oh, well, the dog's got him by now, then," murmured my father, who had heard nothing, and was sleepy.

'"Thomas," replied my mother severely, "I'm not going to lie here while a fellow-creature is being murdered by a savage beast. If you won't go down and save that man's life, I will."

'"Oh, bother," said my father, preparing to get up. "You're always fancying you hear noises. I believe that's all you women come to bed for – to sit up and listen for burglars." Just to satisfy her, however, he pulled on his trousers and socks, and went down.

'Well, sure enough, my mother was right, this time. There *was* a burglar in the house. The pantry window stood open, and a light was shining in the kitchen. My father crept softly forward, and peeped through the partly open door. There sat the burglar, eating cold beef and pickles, and there, beside him, on the floor gazing up into his face with a blood-curdling smile of affection, sat that idiot of a dog, wagging his tail.

'My father was so taken aback that he forgot to keep silent.

'"Well, I'm ——," and he used a word that I should not care to repeat to you fellows.

'The burglar, hearing him, made a dash, and got clear off by the window; and the dog seemed vexed with my father for having driven him away.

'Next morning we took the dog back to the trainer from whom we had bought it.

'"What do you think I wanted this dog for?" asked my father, trying to speak calmly.

'"Well," replied the trainer, "you said you wanted a good house dog."

'"Exactly so," answered the dad. "I didn't ask for a burglar's companion, did I? I didn't say I wanted a dog who'd chum on with a burglar the first time he ever came to the house, and sit with him while he had supper, in case he might feel lonesome, did I?" And my father recounted the incidents of the previous night.

'The man agreed that there was cause for complaint. "I'll tell you what it is, sir," he said. "It was my boy Jim as trained this 'ere dawg, and I guess the young beggar's taught 'im more about tackling rats than burglars. You leave 'im with me for a week, sir; I'll put that all right."

'We did so, and at the end of the time the trainer brought him back again.

'"You'll find 'im game enough now, sir," said the man. "'E ain't what I call an intellectual dawg, but I think I've knocked the right idea into 'im."

'My father thought he'd like to test the matter, so we hired a man for a shilling to break in through the kitchen window while the trainer held the dog by a chain. The dog remained perfectly quiet until the man was fairly inside. Then he made one savage spring at him, and if the chain had not been stout the fellow would have earned his shilling dearly.

'The dad was satisfied now that he could go to bed in peace; and the mater's alarm for the safety of the local burglars was proportionately increased.

'Months passed uneventfully by, and then another burglar sampled our house. This time there could be no doubt that the dog was doing something for his living. The din in the basement was terrific. The house shook with the concussion of falling bodies.

'My father snatched up his revolver and rushed downstairs, and I followed him. The kitchen was in confusion. Tables and chairs were overturned, and on the floor lay a man gurgling

'The trainer brought him back again'

for help. The dog was standing over him, choking him.

'The pater held his revolver to the man's ear, while I, by superhuman effort, dragged our preserver away, and chained him up to the sink, after which I lit the gas.

'Then we perceived that the gentleman on the floor was a police constable.

'"Good heavens!" exclaimed my father, dropping the revolver, "however did you come here?"

'"'Ow did I come 'ere?" retorted the man, sitting up and speaking in a tone of bitter, but not unnatural, indignation. "Why, in the course of my dooty, that's 'ow I come 'ere. I see a burglar getting in through the window, so I just follows and slips in after 'im."

'"Did you catch him?" asked my father.

'"Did I catch 'im!" almost shrieked the man. "'Ow could I catch 'im with that blasted dog of yours 'olding me down by the throat, while 'e lights 'is pipe and walks out by the back door?"

'The dog was for sale the next day. The mater, who had grown to like him, because he let the baby pull his tail, wanted us to keep him. The mistake, she said, was not the animal's fault. Two men broke into the house almost at the same time. The dog could not go for both of them. He did his best, and went for one. That his selection should have fallen upon the policeman instead of upon the burglar was unfortunate. But still it was a thing that might have happened to any dog.

'My father, however, had become prejudiced against the poor creature, and that same week he inserted an advertisement in *The Field*, in which the animal was recommended as an investment likely to prove useful to any enterprising member of the criminal classes.'

MacShaughnassy having had his innings, Jephson took a turn, and told us a pathetic story about an unfortunate mongrel that was run over in the Strand one day and its leg broken. A medical student, who was passing at the time, picked it up and carried it to the Charing Cross Hospital, where its leg was set, and where it was kept and tended until it was quite itself again, when it was sent home.

The poor thing had quite understood what was being done for it, and had been the most grateful patient they had ever had in the hospital. The whole staff were quite sorry when it left.

One morning, a week or two later, the house-surgeon, looking out of the window, saw the dog coming down the street. When it came near he noticed that it had a penny in its mouth. A cat's-meat barrow was standing by the kerb, and for a moment, as he passed it, the dog hesitated.

But his nobler nature asserted itself, and, walking straight up to the hospital railings, and raising himself upon his hind legs, he dropped his penny into the contribution box.

MacShaughnassy was much affected by this story. He said it showed such a beautiful trait in the dog's character. The animal was a poor outcast, vagrant thing, that had perhaps never possessed a penny before in all its life, and might never have another. He said that dog's penny seemed to him to be a greater gift than the biggest cheque that the wealthiest patron ever signed.

The other three were very eager now to get to work on the novel, but I did not quite see the fairness of this. I had one or two dog stories of my own.

I knew a black-and-tan terrier years ago. He lodged in the same house with me. He did not belong to any one. He had discharged his owner (if, indeed, he had ever permitted himself to possess one, which is doubtful, having regard to his aggressively independent character), and was now running himself entirely on his own account. He appropriated the front hall for his sleeping-apartment, and took his meals with the other lodgers – whenever they happened to be having meals.

At five o'clock he would take an early morning snack with young Hollis, an engineer's pupil, who had to get up at half-past four and make his own coffee, so as to be down at the works by six. At eight-thirty he would breakfast in a more sensible fashion with Mr Blair, on the first floor, and on occasions would join Jack Gadbut, who was a late riser, in a devilled kidney at eleven.

From then till about five, when I generally had a cup of tea and a chop, he regularly disappeared. Where he went and what he did between those hours nobody ever knew. Gadbut swore that twice he had met him coming out of a stockbroker's office in Threadneedle Street, and, improbable though the statement at first appeared, some colour of credibility began to attach to it when we reflected upon the dog's inordinate passion for acquiring and hoarding coppers.

This craving of his for wealth was really quite remarkable. He was an elderly dog, with a great sense of his own dignity; yet, on the promise of a penny, I have seen him run round after his own tail until he didn't know one end of himself from the other.

He used to teach himself tricks, and go from room to room in the evening, performing them, and when he had completed his programme he would sit up and beg. All the fellows used to humour him. He must have made pounds in the course of the year.

Once, just outside our door, I saw him standing in a crowd, watching a performing poodle attached to a hurdy-gurdy. The poodle stood on his head, and then, with his hind legs in the air, walked round on his front paws. The people laughed very much, and, when afterwards he came amongst them with his wooden saucer in his mouth, they gave freely.

Our dog came in and immediately commenced to study. In three days *he* could stand on his head and walk round on his front legs, and the first evening he did so he made sixpence. It must have been terribly hard work for him at his age, and subject to rheumatism as he was; but he would do anything for money. I believe he would have sold himself to the devil for eightpence down.

*Standing in a crowd,
watching a performing
poodle*

He knew the value of money. If you held out to him a penny in one hand and a threepenny-bit in the other, he would snatch at the threepence, and then break his heart because he could not get the penny in as well. You might safely have left him in the room with a leg of mutton, but it would not have been wise to leave your purse about.

Now and then he spent a little, but not often. He was desperately fond of sponge-cakes, and occasionally, when he had had a good week, he would indulge himself to the extent of one or two. But he hated paying for them, and always made a frantic and frequently successful effort to get off with the cake and the penny also. His plan of operations was simple. He would walk into the shop with his penny in his mouth, well displayed, and a sweet and lamblike expression in his eyes. Taking his stand as near to the cakes as he could get, and fixing his eyes affectionately upon them, he would begin to whine, and the shopkeeper, thinking he was dealing with an honest dog, would throw him one.

To get the cake he was obliged, of course, to drop the penny, and then began a struggle between him and the shopkeeper for the possession of the coin. The man would try to pick it up. The dog would put his foot upon it, and growl savagely. If he could finish the cake before the contest was over, he would snap up the penny and bolt. I have known him to come home gorged with sponge-cakes, the original penny still in his mouth.

He knew the value of money

So notorious throughout the neighbourhood did this dishonest practice of his become, that, after a time, the majority of the local tradespeople refused to serve him at all. Only the exceptionally quick and able-bodied would attempt to do business with him.

Then he took his custom further afield, into districts where his reputation had not yet penetrated. And he would pick out shops kept by nervous females or rheumatic old men.

They say that the love of money is the root of all evil. It seemed to have robbed him of every shred of principle.

It robbed him of his life in the end, and that came about in this way. He had been performing one evening in Gadbut's room, where a few of us were sitting smoking and talking; and young Hollis, being in a generous mood, had thrown him, as he thought, a sixpence. The dog grabbed it, and retired under the sofa. This was an odd thing for him to do, and we commented upon it. Suddenly a thought occurred to Hollis, and he took out his money and began counting it.

'By Jove,' he exclaimed, 'I've given that little beast half-a-sovereign – here, Tiny!'

But Tiny only backed further underneath the sofa, and no mere verbal invitation would induce him to stir. So we adopted a more pressing plan, and coaxed him out by the scruff of his neck.

He came, an inch at a time, growling viciously, and holding Hollis's half-sovereign tight between his teeth. We tried sweet reasonableness at first. We offered him a sixpence in exchange; he looked insulted, and evidently considered the proposal as tantamount to our calling him a fool. We made it a shilling, then half-a-crown – he seemed only bored by our persistence.

'I don't think you'll ever see this half-sovereign again, Hollis,' said Gadbut, laughing. We all, with the exception of young Hollis, thought the affair a very good joke. He, on the contrary, seemed annoyed, and, taking the dog from Gadbut, make an attempt to pull the coin out of its mouth.

Tiny, true to his life-long principle of never parting if he could possibly help it, held on like grim death, until, feeling that his little earnings were slowly but surely going from him, he made one final desperate snatch, and swallowed the money. It stuck in his throat, and he began to choke.

Then we became seriously alarmed for the dog. He was an amusing chap, and we did not want any accident to happen to him. Hollis rushed into his room and procured a long pair of pincers, and the rest of us held the little miser while Hollis tried to relieve him of the cause of his suffering.

But poor Tiny did not understand our intentions. He still thought we were seeking to rob him of his night's takings, and resisted vehemently. His struggles fixed the coin firmer, and, inspite of our efforts he died – one more victim, among many, to the fierce fever for gold.

Each chest was full of gold

I dreamt a very curious dream about riches once, that made a great impression upon me. I thought that I and a friend – a very dear friend – were living together in a strange old house. I don't think anybody else dwelt in the house but just we two. One day, wandering about this strange old rambling place, I discovered the hidden door of a secret room, and in this room were many iron-bound chests, and when I raised the heavy lids I saw that each chest was full of gold.

And, when I saw this, I stole out softly and closed the hidden door, and drew the worn tapestries in front of it again, and crept back along the dim corridor, looking behind me, fearfully.

And the friend that I had loved came towards me, and we walked together with our hands clasped. But I hated him.

I crawl forward inch by inch

And all day long I kept beside him, or followed him unseen, lest by chance he should learn the secret of that hidden door; and at night I lay awake watching him.

But one night I sleep, and, when I open my eyes, he is no longer near me. I run swiftly up the narrow stairs and along the silent corridor. The tapestry is drawn aside, and the hidden door stands open, and in the room beyond the friend that I loved is kneeling before an open chest, and the glint of the gold is in my eyes.

His back is towards me, and I crawl forward inch by inch. I have a knife in my hand, with a strong, curved blade; and when I am near enough I kill him as he kneels there.

His body falls against the door, and it shuts to with a clang, and I try to open it, and cannot. I beat my hands against its iron nails, and scream, and the dead man grins at me. The light streams in through the chink beneath the massive door, and fades, and comes again, and fades again, and I gnaw at the oaken lids of the iron-bound chests, for the madness of hunger is climbing into my brain.

Then I awake, and find that I really am hungry, and remember that in consequence of a headache I did not eat any dinner. So I slip on a few clothes, and go down to the kitchen on a foraging expedition.

It is said that dreams are momentary conglomerations of thought, centring round the incident that awakens us, and, as with most scientific facts, this is occasionally true. There is one dream that, with slight variations, is continually recurring to me. Over and over again I dream that I am suddenly called upon to act an important part in some piece at the Lyceum. That poor Mr Irving should invariably be the victim seems unfair, but really it is entirely his own fault. It is he who persuades and urges me. I myself would much prefer to remain quietly in bed, and I tell him so. But he insists on my getting up at once and coming down to the theatre. I explain to him that I can't act a bit. He seems to consider this unimportant, and says, 'Oh, that will be all right.' We argue for a while, but he makes the matter quite a personal one, and to oblige him and get him out of the bedroom I consent, though much against my own judgment. I generally dress the character in my nightshirt, though on one occasion, for Banquo, I wore pyjamas, and I never remember a single word of what I ought to say. How I get through I do not know. Irving comes up afterwards and congratulates me, but whether upon the brilliancy of my performance, or upon my luck in getting off the stage before a brickbat is thrown at me, I cannot say.

Whenever I dream this incident I invariably wake up to find that the bedclothes are on the floor, and that I am shivering with cold; and it is this shivering, I suppose, that causes me to dream I am wandering about the Lyceum stage in nothing but my nightshirt. But still I do not understand why it should always be the Lyceum.

Another dream which I fancy I have dreamt more than once – or, if not, I have dreamt that I dreamt it before, a thing one sometimes does – is one in which I am walking down a very wide and very long road in the East End of London. It is a curious road to find there. Omnibuses and trams pass up and down, and it is crowded with stalls and barrows, beside which men in greasy caps stand shouting; yet on each side it is bordered by a strip of tropical forest. The road, in fact, combines the advantages of Kew and Whitechapel.

Some one is with me, but I cannot see him, and we walk through the forest, pushing our way among the tangled vines that cling about our feet, and every now and then, between the giant tree-trunks, we catch glimpses of the noisy street.

At the end of this road there is a narrow turning, and when I come to it I am afraid, though I do not know why I am afraid. It leads to a house that I once lived in when a child, and now there is some one waiting there who has something to tell me.

I turn to run away. A Blackwall 'bus is passing, and I try to overtake it. But the horses turn into skeletons and gallop away from me, and my feet are like lead, and the thing that is with me, and that I cannot see, seizes me by the arm and drags me back.

It forces me along, and into the house, and the door slams to behind us, and the sound echoes through the lifeless rooms. I recognise the rooms; I laughed and cried in them long ago. Nothing is changed. The chairs stand in their places, empty. My mother's knitting lies upon the hearthrug, where the kitten, I remember, dragged it, somewhere back in the sixties.

I go up into my own little attic. My cot stands in the corner, and my bricks lie tumbled out upon the floor (I was always an untidy child). An old man enters – an old, bent, withered man – holding a lamp above his head, and I look at his face, and it is my own face. And another enters, and he also is myself. Then more and more, till the room is thronged with faces, and the stair-way beyond, and all the silent house. Some of the faces are old and others young, and some are fair and smile at me, and many are foul and leer at me. And every face is my own face, but no two of them are alike.

I do not know why the sight of myself should alarm me so, but I rush from the house in terror, and the faces follow me; and I run faster and faster, but I know that I shall never leave them behind me.

As a rule one is the hero of one's own dreams, but at times I have dreamt a dream entirely in the third person – a dream with the incidents of which I have had no connection whatever, except as an unseen and impotent spectator. One of these I have often thought about since, wondering if it could not be worked up into a story. But, perhaps, it would be too painful a theme.

I dreamt I saw a woman's face among a throng. It is an evil face, but there is a strange beauty in it. The flickering gleams thrown by street lamps flash down upon it, showing the wonder of its evil fairness. Then the lights go out I see it next in a place that is very far away, and it is even more beautiful than before, for the evil has gone out of it. Another face is looking down into it, a bright, pure face. The faces meet and kiss, and, as his lips touch hers, the blood mounts to her cheeks and brow. I see the two faces again. But I cannot tell where they are or how long a time has passed. The man's face has grown a little older, but it is still young and fair, and when the woman's eyes rest upon it there comes a glory into her face so that it is like the face of an angel. But at times the woman is alone, and then I see the old evil look struggling back.

Then I see clearer. I see the room in which they live. It is very poor. An old-fashioned piano stands in one corner, and beside it is a table on which lie scattered a tumbled mass of papers round an ink-stand. An empty chair waits before the table. The woman sits by the open window.

From far below there rises the sound of a great city. Its lights throw up faint beams into the dark room. The smell of its streets is in the woman's nostrils.

Every now and again she looks towards the door and listens: then turns to the open window. And I notice that each time she looks towards the door the evil in her face shrinks back; but each time she turns to the window it grows more fierce and sullen.

Suddenly she starts up, and there is a terror in her eyes that frightens me as I dream, and I see great beads of sweat upon her brow. Then, very slowly, her face changes, and I see again the evil creature of the night. She wraps around her an old cloak, and creeps out. I hear her footsteps going down the stairs. They grow fainter and fainter. I hear a door open. The roar of the streets rushes up into the house, and the woman's footsteps are swallowed up.

Time drifts onward through my dream. Scenes change, take shape, and fade; but all is vague and undefined, until, out of the dimness, there fashions itself a long, deserted street. The lights make glistening circles on the wet pavement. A figure, dressed in gaudy rags, slinks by, keeping close against the wall. Its back is towards me, and I do not see its face. Another figure glides from out the shadows. I look upon its face, and I see it is the face that the woman's eyes gazed up into and worshipped

long ago, when
my dream was
just begun. But the
fairness and the purity
are gone from it, and it is old and evil, as the woman's when I
looked upon her last. The figure in the gaudy rags moves
slowly on. The second figure follows it, and overtakes it. The
two pause, and speak to one another as they draw near. The
street is very dark where they have met, and the figure in the
gaudy rags keeps its face still turned aside. They walk together
in silence, till they come to where a flaring gas-lamp hangs
before a tavern; and there the woman turns, and I see that it is
the woman of my dream. And she and the man look into each
other's eyes once more.

In another dream that I remember, an angel (or a devil, I am not quite sure which) has come to a man and told him that so long as he loves no living human thing — so long as he never suffers himself to feel one touch of tenderness towards wife or child, towards kith or kin, towards stranger or towards friend, so long will he succeed and prosper in his dealings — so long will all this world's affairs go well with him; and he will grow each day richer and greater and more powerful. But if ever he let one kindly thought for living thing come into his heart, in that moment all his plans and schemes will topple down about his ears; and from that hour his name will be despised by men, and then forgotten.

And the man treasures up these words, for he is an ambitious man, and wealth and fame and power are the sweetest things in all the world to him. A woman loves him and dies, thirsting for a loving look from him; children's footsteps creep into his life and steal away again, old faces fade and new ones come and go.

But never a kindly touch of his hand rests on any living thing; never a kindly word comes from his lips; never a kindly thought springs from his heart. And in all his doings fortune favours him.

The years pass by, and at last there is left to him only one thing that he need fear — a child's small, wistful face. The child loves him, as the woman, long ago, had loved him, and her eyes follow him with a hungry, beseeching look. But he sets his teeth, and turns away from her.

The little face grows thin, and one day they come to him where he sits before the keyboard of his many enterprises, and tell him she is dying. He comes and stands beside the bed, and the child's eyes open and turn towards him; and, as he draws nearer, her little arms stretch out towards him, pleading dumbly. But the man's face never changes, and the little arms fall feebly back upon the tumbled coverlet, and the wistful eyes grow still, and a woman steps softly forward, and draws the lids down over them; then the man goes back to his plans and schemes.

But in the night, when the great house is silent, he steals up to the room where the child still lies, and pushes back the white, uneven sheet.

'Dead – dead,' he mutters. Then he takes the tiny corpse up in his arms, and holds it tight against his breast, and kisses the cold lips, and the cold cheeks, and the little, cold, stiff hands.

And at that point my story becomes impossible, for I dream that the dead child lies always beneath the sheet in that quiet room, and that little face never changes, nor the limbs decay.

Pleading dumbly

I puzzle about this for an instant, but soon forget to wonder; for when the Dream Fairy tells us tales we are only as little children, sitting round with open eyes, believing all, though marvelling that such things should be.

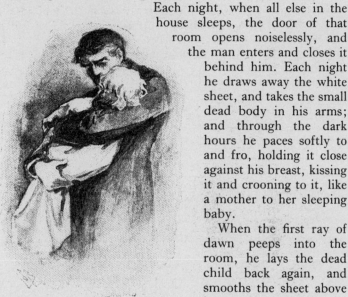

Takes the small dead body in his arms

Each night, when all else in the house sleeps, the door of that room opens noiselessly, and the man enters and closes it behind him. Each night he draws away the white sheet, and takes the small dead body in his arms; and through the dark hours he paces softly to and fro, holding it close against his breast, kissing it and crooning to it, like a mother to her sleeping baby.

When the first ray of dawn peeps into the room, he lays the dead child back again, and smooths the sheet above her, and steals away.

And he succeeds and prospers in all things, and each day he grows richer and greater and more powerful.

CHAPTER III

We had much trouble with our heroine. Brown wanted her ugly. Brown's chief ambition in life is to be original, and his method of obtaining the original is to take the unoriginal and turn it upside down. If Brown were given a little planet of his own to do as he liked with, he would call day, night, and summer, winter. He would make all his men and women walk on their heads and shake hands with their feet, his trees would grow with their roots in the air, and the old cock would lay all the eggs while the hens sat on the fence and crowed. Then he would step back and say, 'See what an original world I have created, entirely my own idea!'

There are many other people besides Brown whose notion of originality would seem to be precisely similar.

I know a little girl, the descendant of a long line of politicians. The hereditary instinct is so strongly developed in her that she is almost incapable of thinking for herself. Instead, she copies in everything her elder sister, who takes more after the mother. If her sister has two helpings of rice pudding for supper, then she has two helpings of rice pudding. If her sister isn't hungry and doesn't want any supper at all, then she goes to bed without any supper.

This lack of character in the child troubles her mother, who is not an admirer of the political virtues, and one evening, taking the little one on her lap, she talked seriously to her.

'Do try to think for yourself,' said she. 'Don't always do just what Jessie does, that's silly. Have an idea of your own now and then. Be a little original.'

The child promised she'd try, and went to bed thoughtful.

Next morning, for breakfast, a dish of kippers and a dish of kidneys were placed on the table, side by side. Now the child loved kippers with an affection that mounted almost to passion, while she loathed kidneys worse than powders. It was the one subject on which she did know her own mind.

'A kidney or a kipper for you, Jessie?' asked the mother, addressing the elder child first.

Jessie hesitated for a moment, while her sister sat regarding her in an agony of suspense.

'Kipper, please, ma,' Jessie answered at last, and the younger child turned her head away to hide the tears.

'You'll have a kipper, of course, Trixy?' said the mother, who had noticed nothing.

'No, thank you, ma,' said the small heroine, stifling a sob, and speaking in a dry, tremulous voice, 'I'll have a kidney.'

'But I thought you couldn't bear kidneys,' exclaimed her mother, surprised.

'No, ma, I don't like 'em much.'

'And you're so fond of kippers!'

'Yes, ma.'

'Well, then, why on earth don't you have one?'

''Cos Jessie's going to have one, and you told me to be original,' and here the poor mite, reflecting upon the price her originality was going to cost her, burst into tears.

The other three of us refused to sacrifice ourselves upon the altar of Brown's originality. We decided to be content with the customary beautiful girl.

'Good or bad?' queried Brown.

'Bad,' responded MacShaughnassy emphatically. 'What do you say, Jephson?'

'Well,' replied Jephson, taking the pipe from between his lips, and speaking in that soothingly melancholy tone of voice that he never varies, whether telling a joke about a wedding or an anecdote relating to a funeral, 'not altogether bad. Bad, with good instincts, the good instincts well under control.'

'I wonder why it is,' murmured MacShaughnassy reflectively, 'that bad people are so much more interesting than good.'

'I don't think the reason is very difficult to find,' answered Jephson. 'There's more uncertainty about them. They keep you more on the alert. It's like the difference between riding a well-broken, steady-going hack and a lively young colt with ideas of his own. The one is comfortable to travel on, but the other provides you with more exercise. If you start off with a thoroughly good woman

for your heroine you give your story away in the first chapter. Everybody knows precisely how she will behave under every conceivable combination of circumstances in which you can place her. On every occasion she will do the same thing – that is, the right thing.

'With a bad heroine, on the other hand, you can never be quite sure what is going to happen. Out of the fifty or so courses open to her, she may take the right one, or she may take one of the forty-nine wrong ones, and you watch her with curiosity to see which it will be.'

'But surely there are plenty of good heroines who are interesting,' I said.

'At intervals – when they do something wrong,' answered Jephson. 'A consistently irreproachable heroine is as irritating as Socrates must have been to Xantippe, or as the model boy at school is to all the other lads. Take the stock heroine of the eighteenth-century romance. She never met her lover except for the purpose of telling him that she could not be his, and she generally wept steadily throughout the interview. She never forgot to turn pale at the sight of blood, nor to faint in his arms at the most inconvenient moment possible. She was determined never to marry without her father's consent, and was equally resolved never to marry anybody but the one particular person she was convinced he would never agree to her marrying. She was an excellent young woman, and nearly as uninteresting as a celebrity at home.'

'Ah, but you're not talking about good women now,' I observed. 'You're talking about some silly person's idea of a good woman.'

'I quite admit it,' replied Jephson. 'Nor, indeed, am I prepared to say what is a good woman. I consider the subject too deep and too complicated for any mere human being to give judgment upon. But I *am* talking of the women who conformed to the popular idea of maidenly goodness in the age when these books were written. You must remember goodness is not a known quantity. It varies with every age and every locality, and it is, generally speaking, your "silly persons" who are responsible for its varying standards. In Japan, a "good" girl would be a girl who would sell her honour in order to afford little luxuries to her aged parents. In certain hospitable

52

islands of the torrid zone, the "good" wife goes to lengths that we should deem altogether unnecessary in making her husband's guest feel himself at home. In ancient Hebraic days, Jael was accounted a good woman for murdering a sleeping man, and Sarai stood in no danger of losing the respect of her little world when she led Hagar unto Abraham. In eighteenth-century England, supernatural stupidity and dulness of a degree that must have been difficult to attain, were held to be feminine virtues – indeed, they are so still – and authors, who are always among the most servile followers of public opinion, fashioned their puppets accordingly. Nowadays "slumming" is the most applauded virtue, and so all our best heroines go slumming, and are "good to the poor."'

*'The most inconvenient
moment possible'*

'How useful "the poor" are,' remarked MacShaughnassy, somewhat abruptly, placing his feet on the mantelpiece, and tilting his chair back till it stood at an angle that caused us to rivet our attention upon it with hopeful interest. 'I don't think we scribbling fellows ever fully grasp how much we owe to "the poor". Where would our angelic heroines and our noble-hearted heroes be if it were not for "the poor"? We want to show that the dear girl is as good as she is beautiful. What do we do? We put a basket full of chickens and bottles of wine on her arm, a fetching little sun-bonnet on her head, and send her round among the poor. How do we prove that our apparent scamp of a hero is really a noble young man at heart? Why, by explaining that he is good to the poor.

'They are as useful in real life as they are in Bookland. What is it consoles the tradesman when the actor, earning eighty pounds a week, cannot pay his debts? Why, reading in the theatrical newspapers gushing accounts of the dear fellow's invariable generosity to the poor. What is it stills the small but irritating voice of conscience when we have successfully accomplished some extra big feat of swindling? Why, the noble resolve to give ten per cent of the net profits to the poor.

'What does a man do when he finds himself growing old, and feels that it is time for him to think seriously about securing his position in the next world? Why, he becomes suddenly good to the poor. If the poor were not there for him to be good to, what could he do? He would be unable to reform at all. It's a great comfort to think that the poor will always be with us. They are the ladder by which we climb into heaven.'

There was silence for a few moments, while MacShaughnassy puffed away vigorously, and almost savagely, at his pipe, and then Brown said: 'I can tell you rather a quaint incident, bearing very aptly on the subject. A cousin of mine was a land-agent in a small country town, and among the houses on his list was a fine old mansion that had remained vacant for many years. He had despaired of ever selling it, when one day an elderly lady, very richly dressed, drove up to the office and

'All our best heroines go slumming'

made inquiries about it. She said she had come across it accidentally while travelling through that part of the country the previous autumn, and had been much struck by its beauty and picturesqueness. She added she was looking out for some quiet spot where she could settle down and peacefully pass the remainder of her days, and thought this place might possibly prove to be the very thing for her.

'My cousin, delighted with the chance of a purchaser, at once drove her across to the estate, which was about eight miles distant from the town, and they went over it together. My cousin waxed eloquent upon the subject of its advantages. He dwelt upon its quiet and seclusion, its proximity – but not too close proximity – to the church, its convenient distance from the village.

'What class of poor have you got round about?'

'Everything pointed to a satisfactory conclusion of business. The business. The lady was charmed with the situation and the surroundings, and delighted with the house and grounds. She considered the price moderate.

'"And now, Mr Brown," said she, as they stood by the lodge gate, "tell me, what class of poor have you got round about?"

'"Poor?" answered my cousin; "there are no poor."

'"No poor!" exclaimed the lady. "No poor people in the village, or anywhere near?"

'"You won't find a poor person within five miles of the

estate," he replied proudly. "You see, my dear madam, this is a thinly populated and exceedingly prosperous county: this particular district especially so. There is not a family in it that is not, comparatively speaking, well-to-do."

"'I'm sorry to hear that," said the lady, in a tone of disappointment. "That place would have suited me so admirably but for that."

"'But surely, madam," cried my cousin, to whom a demand for poor persons was an entirely new idea, "you don't mean to say that you *want* poor people! Why, we've always considered it one of the chief attractions of the property – nothing to shock the eye or wound the susceptibilities of the most tender-hearted occupant."

"'My dear Mr Brown," replied the lady, "I will be perfectly frank with you. I am becoming an old woman, and my past life has not, perhaps, been altogether too well spent. It is my desire to atone for the – er – follies of my youth by an old age of well-doing, and to that end it is essential that I should be surrounded by a certain number of deserving poor. I had hoped to find in this charming neighbourhood of yours the customary proportion of poverty and misery, in which case I should have taken the house without hesitation. As it is, I must seek elsewhere."

'My cousin was perplexed, and sad. "There are plenty of poor people in the town," he said, "many of them most interesting cases, and you could have the entire care of them all. There'd be no opposition whatever, I'm positive."

"'Thank you," replied the lady, "but I really couldn't go as far as the town. They must be within easy driving distance or they are no good."

'My cousin cudgelled his brains again. He did not intend to let a purchaser slip through his fingers if he could help it. At last a bright thought flashed into his mind. "I'll tell you what we could do," he said. "There's a piece of waste land the other end of the village that we've never been able to do much with, in consequence of its being so swampy. If you liked, we could run you up a dozen cottages on that, cheap – it would be all the better their being a bit ramshackle and unhealthy – and get some poor people for you, and put into them."

'The lady reflected upon the idea, and it struck her as a good one.

'"You see," continued my cousin, pushing his advantage, "by adopting this method you would be able to select your own poor. We would get you some nice, clean, grateful poor, and make the thing pleasant for you."

'It ended in the lady's accepting my cousin's offer, and giving him a list of the poor people she would like to have. She selected one bedridden old woman (Church of England preferred); one paralytic old man; one blind girl who would want to be read aloud to; one poor atheist, willing to be converted; two cripples; one drunken father who would consent to be talked to seriously; one disagreeable old fellow, needing much patience; two large families, and four ordinary assorted couples.

'My cousin experienced some difficulty in securing the drunken father. Most of the drunken fathers he interviewed upon the subject had a rooted objection to being talked to at all. After a long search, however, he discovered a mild little man, who, upon the lady's requirements and charitable intentions being explained to him, undertook to qualify himself for the vacancy by getting intoxicated at least once a week. He said he could not promise more than once a week at first, he unfortunately possessing a strong natural distaste for all alcoholic liquors, which it would be necessary for him to overcome. As he got more used to them, he would do better.

'Over the disagreeable old man, my cousin also had trouble. It was hard to hit the right degree of disagreeableness. Some of them were so very unpleasant. He eventually made choice of a decayed cab-driver with advanced Radical opinions, who insisted on a three years' contract.

'The plan worked exceedingly well, and does so, my cousin tells me, to this day. The drunken father has completely conquered his dislike to strong drink. He has not been sober now for over three weeks, and has lately taken to knocking his wife about. The disagreeable fellow is most conscientious in fulfilling his part of the bargain, and makes himself a perfect curse to the whole village. The others have dropped into their respective positions and are working well. The lady visits them all every afternoon, and is most charitable. They call her Lady Bountiful, and everybody blesses her.'

Brown rose as he finished speaking, and mixed himself a glass of whisky and water with the self-satisfied air of a benevolent man about to reward somebody for having done a good deed; and MacShaughnassy lifted up his voice and talked.

'I know a story bearing on the subject, too,' he said. 'It happened in a tiny Yorkshire village – a peaceful, respectable spot, where folks found life a bit slow. One day, however, a new curate arrived, and that woke things up considerably. He was a nice young man, and, having a large private income of his own, was altogether a most desirable catch. Every unmarried female in the place went for him with one accord.

'But ordinary feminine blandishments appeared to have no effect upon him. He was a seriously inclined young man, and once, in the course of a casual conversation upon the subject of love, he was heard to say that he himself should never be attracted by mere beauty and charm. What would appeal to him, he said, would be a woman's goodness – her charity and kindliness to the poor.

'With a private income of his own'

'Well, that set the petticoats all thinking. They saw that in studying fashion plates and practising expressions they had been going upon the wrong tack. The card for them to play was "the poor."

'But here a serious difficulty arose. There was only one poor person in the whole parish, a cantankerous old fellow who lived in a tumble-down cottage at the back of the church, and fifteen able-bodied women (eleven girls, three old maids, and a widow) wanted to be "good" to him.

'Miss Simmonds, one of the old maids, got hold of him first, and commenced feeding him twice a day with beef-tea; and then the widow boarded him with port wine and oysters. Later in the week others of the party drifted in upon him, and wanted to cram him with jelly and chickens.

'The old man couldn't understand it. He was accustomed to a small sack of coals now and then, accompanied by a long lecture on his sins, and an occasional bottle of dandelion tea. This sudden spurt on the part of Providence puzzled him. He said nothing, however, but continued to take in as much of everything as he could hold. At the end of a month he was too fat to get through his own back door.

'The competition among the women-folk grew keener every day, and at last the old man began to give himself airs, and to make the place hard for them. He made them clean his cottage out, and cook his meals, and when he was tired of having them about the house, he set them to work in the garden.

'They grumbled a good deal, and there was a talk at one time of a sort of a strike, but what could they do? He was the only pauper for miles round, and knew it. He had the monopoly, and, like all monopolists, he abused his position.

'He made them run errands. He sent them out to buy his "baccy," at their own expense. On one occasion he sent Miss Simmonds out with a jug to get his supper beer. She indignantly refused at first, but he told her that if she gave him any of her stuck-up airs out she would go, and never come into his house again. If she wouldn't do it there were plenty of others who would. She knew it and went.

'They had been in the habit of reading to him – good books with an elevating tendency. But now he put his foot down upon that sort of thing. He said he didn't want Sunday-school rubbish at his time of life. What he liked was something spicy. And he made them read him French novels and seafaring tales, containing realistic language. And they didn't have to skip anything either, or he'd know the reason why.

'He said he liked music, so a few of them clubbed together and bought him a harmonium. Their idea was that they would

'With chorus and skirt dance'

sing hymns and play high-class melodies, but it wasn't his. His idea was – "Keeping up the old girl's birthday" and "She winked the other eye," with chorus and skirt dance, and that's what they sang.

'To what lengths his tyranny would have gone it is difficult to say, had not an event happened that brought his power to a premature collapse. This was the curate's sudden and somewhat unexpected marriage with a very beautiful burlesque actress who had lately been performing in a neighbouring town. He gave up the Church on his engagement, in consequence of his *fiancée's* objection to becoming a minister's wife. She said she could never "tumble to" the district visiting.

'With the curate's wedding the old pauper's brief career of prosperity ended. They packed him off to the workhouse after that, and made him break stones.'

At the end of the telling of his tale, MacShaughnassy lifted his feet off the mantelpiece, and set to work to wake up his legs; and Jephson took a hand, and began to spin us stories.

But none of us felt inclined to laugh at Jephson's stories, for they dealt not with the goodness of the rich to the poor, which is a virtue yielding quick and highly satisfactory returns, but with the goodness of the poor to the poor, a somewhat less remunerative investment and a different matter altogether.

For the poor themselves – I do not mean the noisy professional poor, but the silent, fighting poor – one is bound to feel a genuine respect. One honours them, as one honours a wounded soldier.

In the perpetual warfare between Humanity and Nature, the poor stand always in the van. They die in the ditches, and we march over their bodies with the flags flying and the drums playing.

One cannot think of them without an uncomfortable feeling that one ought to be a little bit ashamed of living in security and ease, leaving them to take all the hard blows. It is as if one were always skulking in the tents, while one's comrades were fighting and dying in the front.

They bleed and fall in silence there. Nature with her terrible club, 'Survival of the Fittest'; and Civilisation with her cruel sword, 'Supply and Demand,' beat them back, and they give way inch by inch, fighting to the end. But it is in a dumb, sullen way, that is not sufficiently picturesque to be heroic.

I remember seeing an old bull-dog, one Saturday night, lying on the doorstep of a small shop in the New Cut. He lay there very quiet, and seemed a bit sleepy; and, as he looked savage, nobody disturbed him. People stepped in and out over him, and occasionally in doing so, one would accidentally kick him, and then he would breathe a little harder and quicker.

At last a passer-by, feeling something wet beneath his feet, looked down, and found that he was standing in a pool of blood, and, looking to see where it came from, found that it flowed in a thick, dark stream from the step on which the dog was lying.

Then he stooped down and examined the dog, and the dog opened its eyes sleepily and looked at him, gave a grin which may have implied pleasure, or may have implied irritation at being disturbed, and died.

A crowd collected, and they turned the dead body of the dog over on its side, and saw a fearful gash in the groin, out of which oozed blood, and other things. The proprietor of the shop said the animal had been there for over an hour.

I have known the poor to die in that same grim, silent way – not the poor that you, my delicately-gloved Lady Bountiful and my very excellent Sir Simon DoGood, know, or that you would care to know; not the poor who march in processions with banners and collection-boxes; not the poor that clamour round your soup kitchens and sing hymns at your tea meetings; but the poor that you don't know are poor until the tale is told at the coroner's inquest – the silent, proud poor who wake each morning to wrestle with Death till night-time, and who, when at last he overcomes them, and, forcing them down on the rotting floor of the dim attic, strangles them, still die with their teeth tight shut.

There was a boy I came to know when I was living in the East End of London. He was not a nice boy by any means. He was not quite so clean as are the good boys in the religious magazines, and I have known a sailor to stop him in the street and reprove him for using indelicate language.

He and his mother and the baby, a sickly infant of about five months old, lived in a cellar down a turning off Three Colt Street. I am not quite sure what had become of the father. I rather think he had been 'converted', and had gone off round the country on a preaching tour. The lad earned six shillings a week as an errand-boy; and the mother stitched trousers, and on days when she was feeling strong and energetic would often make as much as tenpence, or even a shilling. Unfortunately, there were days when the four bare walls would chase each other round and round, and the candle seem a faint speck of light, a very long way off; and the frequency of these caused the family income for the week to occasionally fall somewhat low.

One night the walls danced round quicker and quicker till they danced away altogether, and the candle shot up through the ceiling and became a star; and the woman knew that it was time to put away her sewing.

'Jim,' she said: she spoke very low, and the boy had to bend over her to hear, 'if you poke about in the middle of the mattress you'll find a couple of pounds. I saved them up a long while ago. That will pay for burying me. And, Jim, you'll take care of the kid. You won't let it go to the parish.'

Jim promised.

'Say "S'welp me Gawd," Jim.'

'S'welp me Gawd, mother.'

Then the woman, having arranged her worldly affairs, lay back ready, and Death struck.

Jim kept his oath. He found the money, and buried his mother; and then, putting his household goods on a barrow, moved into cheaper apartments – half an old shed, for which he paid two shillings a week.

For eighteen months he and the baby lived there. He left the child at a nursery every morning, fetching it away each evening on his return from work, and for that he paid fourpence a day, which included a limited supply of milk. How he managed to keep himself and more than half keep the child on the remaining two shillings I cannot say. I only know that he did it, and that not a soul ever helped him or knew that there was help wanted. He nursed the child, often pacing the room with it for hours, washed it, occasionally, and took it out for an airing every Sunday.

Notwithstanding all which care, the little beggar, at the end of the time above mentioned, 'pegged out,' to use Jimmy's own words.

The coroner was very severe on Jim. 'If you had taken proper steps,' he said, 'this child's life might have been preserved.' (He seemed to think it would have been better if the child's life had been preserved. Coroners have quaint ideas!) 'Why didn't you apply to the relieving officer?'

''Cos I didn't want no relief,' replied Jim sullenly. 'I promised my mother it should never go on the parish, and it didn't.'

The incident occurred, very luckily, during the dead season, and the evening papers took the case up, and made rather a good thing out of it. Jim became quite a hero, I remember. Kind-hearted people wrote, urging that somebody – the ground landlord, or the Government, or some one of that sort – ought to do something for him. And everybody abused the local vestry. I really think some benefit to Jim might have come out of it all if only the excitement had lasted a little longer. Unfortunately, however, just at its height a spicy divorce case cropped up, and Jim was crowded out and forgotten.

I told the boys this story of mine, after Jephson had done telling his, and, when I had finished, we found it was nearly one o'clock. So, of course, it was too late to do any more work to the novel that evening.

CHAPTER IV

We held our next business meeting on my houseboat. Brown was opposed at first to my going down to this houseboat at all. He thought that none of us should leave town while the novel was still on hand.

MacShaughnassy, on the contrary, was of opinion that we should work better on a houseboat. Speaking for himself, he said he never felt more like writing a really great work than when lying in a hammock among whispering leaves, with the deep blue sky above him, and a tumbler of iced claret cup within easy reach of his hand. Failing a hammock, he found a deck chair a great incentive to mental labour. In the interests of the novel, he strongly recommended me to take down with me at least one comfortable deck chair, and plenty of lemons.

Writing a really great work

I could not myself see any reason why we should not be able to think as well on a houseboat as anywhere else, and accordingly it was settled that I should go down and establish myself upon the thing, and that the others should visit me there from time to time, when we would sit round and toil.

This houseboat was Ethelbertha's idea. We had spent a day, the summer before, on one belonging to a friend of mine, and she had been enraptured with the life. Everything was on such a delightfully tiny scale. You lived in a tiny little room; you slept on a tiny little bed, in a tiny, tiny little bedroom; and you cooked your little dinner by a tiny little fire, in the tiniest little kitchen that ever you did see. 'Oh, it must be lovely, living on a houseboat,' said Ethelbertha, with a gasp of ecstasy; 'it must be like living in a doll's house.'

Ethelbertha was very young – ridiculously young, as I think I have mentioned before – in those days of which I am writing, and the love of dolls, and of the gorgeous dresses that dolls wear, and of the many-windowed but inconveniently arranged houses that dolls inhabit – or are supposed to inhabit, for as a rule they seem to prefer sitting on the roof with their legs dangling down over the front door, which has always appeared to me to be unladylike: but then, of course, I am no authority on doll eti- quette – had not yet, I think, quite depar- ted from her. Nay, am I not sure that it had not? Do I not remember, years later, peeping into a certain room, the

Sitting on the floor, before a red brick mansion

walls of which are covered with works of art of a character calculated to send any aesthetic person mad, and seeing her, sitting on the floor, before a red brick mansion, containing two rooms and a kitchen; and are not her hands trembling with delight as she arranges the three real tin plates upon the dresser? And does she not knock at the real brass knocker upon the real front door until it comes off, and I have to sit down beside her on the floor and screw it on again?

Perhaps, however, it is unwise for me to recall these things, and bring them forward thus in evidence against her, for cannot she in turn laugh at me? Did not I also assist in the arrangement and appointment of that house beautiful? We differed on the matter of the drawing-room carpet, I recollect. Ethelbertha fancied a dark blue velvet, but I felt sure, taking the wallpaper into consider-

*Ethelbertha fancied a
dark blue velvet*

ation, that some shade of terra-cotta would harmonise best. She agreed with me in the end, and we manufactured one out of an old chest protector. It had a really charming effect, and gave a delightfully warm tone to the room. The blue velvet we put in the kitchen. I deemed this extravagance, but Ethelbertha said that servants thought a lot of a good carpet, and that it paid to humour them in little things, when practicable.

The bedroom had one big bed and a cot in it; but I could not see where the girl was going to sleep. The architect had overlooked her altogether: that is so like an architect. The house also suffered from the inconvenience common to residences of its class, of possessing no stairs, so that to move from one room to another it was necessary to burst your way up through the ceiling, or else to come outside and climb in through a window; either of which methods must be fatiguing when you come to do it often.

Apart from these drawbacks, however, the house was one that any doll agent would have been justified in describing as a 'most desirable family residence'; and it had been furnished with a lavishness that bordered on positive ostentation. In the bedroom there was a washing-stand, and on the washing-stand there stood a jug and basin, and in the jug there was real water. But all this was as nothing. I have known mere ordinary, middle-class dolls' houses in which you might find washing-stands and jugs and basins and real water – ay, and even soap. But in this abode of luxury there was a real towel; so that a body could not only wash himself, but wipe himself afterwards, and that is a sensation that, as all dolls know, can be enjoyed only in the very first-class establishments.

Then, in the drawing-room, there was a clock, which would tick just so long as you continued to shake it (it never seemed to get tired); also a picture and a piano, and a book upon the table, and a vase of flowers that would upset the moment you touched it, just like a real vase of flowers. Oh, there was style about this room, I can tell you.

But the glory of the house was its kitchen. There were all things that heart could desire in this kitchen, saucepans with lids that took on and off, a flat-iron and a rolling-pin. A dinner service for three occupied about half the room, and what space was left was filled up by the stove – a *real* stove! Think of it, oh ye owners of dolls' houses, a stove in which you could burn real bits of coal, and on which you could boil real bits of potato for dinner – except when people said you mustn't, because it was dangerous, and took the grate away from you, and blew out the fire, a thing that hampers a cook.

I never saw a house more complete in all its details. Nothing had been overlooked, not even the family. It lay on its back, just outside the front door, proud but calm, waiting to be put into possession. It was not an extensive family. It consisted of four – papa, and mamma, and baby, and the hired girl; just the family for a beginner.

It was a well-dressed family too – not merely with grand clothes outside, covering a shameful condition of things beneath, such as, alas! is too often the case in doll society, but with every article necessary and proper to a lady or gentleman, down to items that I could not mention. And all these garments, you must know, could be unfastened and taken off. I have known dolls – stylish enough dolls, to look at, some of them – who have been content to go about with their clothes gummed on to them, and in some cases, nailed on with tacks, which I take to be a slovenly and unhealthy habit. But this family could be undressed in five minutes without the aid of either hot water or a chisel.

Not that it was advisable from an artistic point of view that any of them should. They had not the figure that looks well in its natural state – none of them. There was a want of fulness about them all. Besides, without their clothes, it might have been difficult to distinguish the baby from the papa, or the maid from the mistress, and thus domestic complications might have arisen.

When all was ready for their reception we established them in their home. We put as much of the baby to bed as the cot would hold, and made the papa and mamma comfortable in the drawing-room, where they sat on the floor and stared thoughtfully at each other across the table. (They had to sit on the floor because the chairs were not big enough.) The girl we placed in the kitchen, where she leant against the dresser in an attitude suggestive of drink, embracing the broom we had given her with maudlin affection. Then we lifted up the house with care, and carried it cautiously into another room, and with the deftness of experienced conspirators placed it the foot of a small bed, on the south-west corner of which an absurdly small somebody had hung an absurdly small stocking.

To return to our own doll's house, Ethelbertha and I, discussing the subject during our return journey in the train, resolved that, next year, we ourselves would possess a houseboat, a smaller houseboat, if possible, than even the one we had just seen. It should have art-muslin curtains and a flag, and the flowers about it should be wild roses and forget-me-nots. I could work all the morning on the roof, with an awning over me to keep off the sun, while Ethelbertha trimmed the roses and made cakes for tea; and in the evenings we would sit out on the little deck, and Ethelbertha would play the guitar (she would begin learning it at once), or we could sit quiet and listen to the nightingales.

For, when you are very, very young you dream that the summer is all sunny days and moonlight nights, that the wind blows always softly from the west, and that roses will thrive anywhere. But, as you grow older, you grow tired of waiting for the gray sky to break. So you close the door and come in, and crouch over the fire, wondering why the winds blow over from the east: and you have given up trying to rear roses.

I knew a little cottage girl who saved up her money for months and months so as to buy a new frock in which to go to a flower-show. But the day of the flower-show was a wet day, so she wore an old frock instead. And all the fête days for quite a long while were wet days, and she feared she would never have a chance of wearing her pretty white dress. But at last there came a fête day morning that was bright and sunny, and then the little girl clapped her hands and ran upstairs, and took her new frock (which had been her 'new frock' for so long a time that it was now the oldest frock she had) from the box where it lay neatly folded between lavender and thyme, and held it up, and laughed to think how nice she would look in it.

But when she went to put it on, she found that she had

out-grown it, and that it was too small for her every way. So she had to wear a common old frock after all.

Things happen that way, you know, in this world. There were a boy and girl once who loved each other very dearly. But they were both poor, so they agreed to wait till he had made enough money for them to live comfortably upon, and then they would marry and be happy. It took him a long while to make, because making money is very slow work, and he wanted, while he was about it, to make enough for them to be very happy upon indeed. He accomplished the task eventually, however, and came back home a wealthy man.

Then they met again in the poorly-furnished parlour where they had parted. But they did not sit as near to each other as of old. For she had lived alone so long that she had grown old-maidish, and she was feeling vexed with him for having dirtied the carpet with his muddy boots. And he had worked so long earning money that he had grown hard and cold like the money itself, and was trying to think of something affectionate to say to her.

They met again

So for a while they sat, one each side of the paper 'fire-stove ornament,' both wondering why they had shed such scalding tears on that day they had kissed each other good-bye; then said 'good-bye' again, and were glad.

There is another tale with much the same moral that I learnt at school out of a copy-book. If I remember rightly, it runs somewhat like this:—

Once upon a time there lived a wise grasshopper and a foolish ant. All through the pleasant summer weather the grasshopper sported and played, gambolling with his fellows in and out among the sun-beams, dining sumptuously each day on the leaves and dew-drops, never troubling about the morrow, singing ever his one peaceful, droning song.

But there came the cruel winter, and the grasshopper, looking around, saw that his friends, the flowers, lay dead, and knew thereby that his own little span was drawing near its close.

Then he felt glad that he had been so happy, and had not wasted his life. 'It has been very short,' said he to himself; 'but it has been very pleasant, and I think I have made the best use of it. I have drunk in the sunshine, I have lain on the soft, warm air, I have played merry games in the waving grass, I have tasted the juice of the sweet green leaves. I have done what I could. I have spread my wings, I have sung my song. Now I will thank God for the sunny days that are passed, and die.'

Saying which, he crawled under a brown leaf, and met his fate in the way that all brave grasshoppers should; and a little bird that was passing by picked him up tenderly and buried him.

Now when the foolish ant saw this, she was greatly puffed up with Pharisaical conceit. 'How thankful I ought to be,' said she, 'that I am industrious and prudent, and not like this poor grasshopper. While he was flitting about from flower to flower, enjoying himself, I was hard at work, putting by against the winter. Now he is dead, while I am about to make myself cosy in my warm home, and eat all the good things that I have been saving up.'

But, as she spoke, the gardener came along with his spade, and levelled the hill where she dwelt to the ground, and left her lying dead amidst the ruins.

Then the same kind little bird that had buried the grasshopper came and picked her out and buried her also; and afterwards he composed and sang a song, the burthen of which was, 'Gather ye rosebuds while ye may.' It was a very pretty song, and a very wise song, and a man who lived in those days, and to whom the birds, loving him and feeling that he was almost one of themselves, had taught their language, fortunately overheard it and wrote it down, so that all may read it to this day.

Buried him

Unhappily for us, however, Fate is a harsh governess, who has no sympathy with our desire for rosebuds. 'Don't stop to pick flowers now, my dear,' she cries, in her sharp, cross tones, as she seizes our arm and jerks us back into the roadway; 'we haven't time to-day. We will come back again to-morrow, and you shall pick them then.'

And we have to follow her, knowing, if we are experienced children, that the chances are that we shall never come that way to-morrow; or that, if we do, the roses will be dead.

Fate would not hear of our having a houseboat that summer, – which was an exceptionally fine summer, – but promised us that if we were good and saved up our money, we should have one next year; and Ethelbertha and I being simple-minded, inexperienced children, were content with the promise, and had faith in its satisfactory fulfilment.

As soon as we reached home we informed Amenda of our plan. The moment the girl opened the door, Ethelbertha burst out with:–

'Oh! can you swim, Amenda?'

'No, mum,' answered Amenda, with entire absence of curiosity as to why such a question had been addressed to her. 'I never knew but one girl as could, and she got drowned.'

'Well, you'll have to make haste and learn, then,' continued Ethelbertha, 'because you won't be able to walk out with your young man, you'll have to swim out. We're not going to live in a house any more. We're going to live on a boat in the middle of the river.'

Ethelbertha's chief object in life at this period was to surprise and shock Amenda, and her chief sorrow that she had never succeeded in doing so. She had hoped great things from this announcement, but the girl remained unmoved. 'Oh, are you, mum,' she replied; and went on to speak of other matters.

'Can you swim, Amenda?'

I believe the result would have been the same if we had told her we were going to live in a balloon.

I do not know how it was, I am sure. Amenda was always most respectful in her manner. But she had a knack of making Ethelbertha and myself feel that we were a couple of children, playing at being grown up and married, and that she was humouring us.

Amenda stayed with us for nearly five years – until the milkman, having saved up sufficient to buy a 'walk' of his own, had become practicable – but her attitude towards us never changed. Even when we came to be really important married people, the proprietors of a 'family', it was evident that she merely considered we had gone a step further in the game, and were playing now at being fathers and mothers.

By some subtle process she contrived to imbue the baby also with this idea. The child never seemed to me to take either of us quite seriously. She would play with us, or join with us in light conversation; but when it came to the serious affairs of life, such as bathing or feeding, she preferred her nurse.

Ethelbertha attempted to take her out in the perambulator one morning, but the child would not hear of it for a moment.

'It's all right baby dear,' explained Ethelbertha soothingly. 'Baby's going out with mamma this morning.'

'Oh no, baby ain't,' was baby's rejoinder, in effect if not in words. 'Baby don't take a hand in experiments – not this baby. I don't want to be upset or run over.'

Poor Ethel! I shall never forget how heart-broken she was. It was the want of confidence that wounded her.

But these are reminiscences of other days, having no connection with the days of which I am – or should be – writing; and to wander from one matter to another is, in a teller of tales, a grievous sin, and a growing custom much to be condemned. Therefore I will close my eyes to all other memories, and endeavour to see only that little white and green houseboat by the ferry, which was the scene of our future collaborations.

Houseboats then were not built to the scale of Mississippi steamers, but this boat was a small one, even for that primitive age. The man from whom we hired it described it as 'compact.' • The man to whom, at the end of the first month, we tried to sub-let it, characterised it as 'poky.' In our letters we traversed this definition. In our hearts we agreed with it.

At first, however, its size – or, rather, its lack of size – was one of its chief charms in Ethelbertha's eyes. The fact that if you got out of bed carelessly you were certain to knock your head against the ceiling, and that is was utterly impossible for any man to put on his trousers except in the saloon, she regarded as a capital joke.

That she herself had to take a looking-glass and go upon the roof to do her back hair, she thought less amusing.

Amenda accepted her new surroundings with her usual philosophic indifference. On being informed that what she had mistaken for a linen-press was her bedroom, she remarked that there was one advantage about it, and that was, that she could not tumble out of bed, seeing there was nowhere to tumble; and, on being shown the kitchen, she observed that she should like it for two things – one was that she could sit in the middle and reach everything without getting up; the other, that nobody else could come into the apartment while she was there.

'You see, Amenda,' explained Ethelbertha apologetically, 'we shall really live live outside.'

'Yes, mum,' answered Amenda, 'I should say that would be the best place to do it.'

If only we could have lived more outside, the life might have been pleasant enough, but the weather rendered it impossible, six days out of the seven, for us to do more than look out of the window and feel thankful that we had a roof over our heads.

I have known wet summers before and since. I have learnt

by many bitter experiences the danger and foolishness of leaving the shelter of London any time between the first of May and the thirty-first of October. Indeed, the country is always associated in my mind with recollections of long, weary days passed in the pitiless rain, and sad evenings spent in other people's clothes. But never have I known, and never, I pray night and morning, may I know again, such a summer as the one we lived through (though none of us expected to) on that confounded houseboat.

In the morning we would be awakened by the rain's forcing its way through the window and wetting the bed, and would get up and mop out the saloon. After breakfast I would try to work, but the beating of the hail upon the roof just over my head would drive every idea out of my brain, and, after a wasted hour or two, I would fling down my pen and hunt up Ethelbertha, and we would put on our mackintoshes and take our umbrellas and go out for a row. At mid-day we would return and put on some dry clothes, and sit down to dinner.

In the afternoon the storm generally freshened up a bit, and we were kept pretty busy rushing about with towels and cloths, trying to prevent the water from coming into the rooms and swamping us. During tea-time the saloon was usually illuminated by forked lightning. The evenings we spent in baling out the boat, after which we took it in turns to go into the kitchen and warm ourselves. At eight we supped, and from then until it was time to go to bed we sat wrapped up in rugs, listening to the roaring of the thunder, and the howling of the wind, and the lashing of the waves, and wondering whether the boat would hold out through the night.

Friends would come down to spend the day with us – elderly, irritable people, fond of warmth and comfort; people who did not, as a rule, hanker after jaunts, even under the most favourable conditions; but who had been persuaded by our silly talk that a day on the river would be to them like a Saturday to Monday in Paradise.

They would arrive soaked; and we would shut them up in different bunks, and leave them to strip themselves and put on things of Ethelbertha's or of mine. But Ethel and I, in those days, were slim, so that stout, middle-aged people in our clothes neither looked well nor felt happy.

Upon their emerging we would take them into the saloon and try to entertain them by telling them what we had intended to do with them had the day been fine. But their answers were short, and occasionally snappy, and after a while the conversation would flag, and we would sit round reading last week's newspapers and coughing.

The moment their own clothes were dry (we lived in a perpetual atmosphere of steaming clothes) they would insist upon leaving us, which seemed to me discourteous after all that we had done for them, and would dress themselves once more and start off home, and get wet again before they got there.

We would generally receive a letter a few days afterwards, written by some relative, informing us that both patients were doing as well as could be expected, and promising to send us a card for the funeral in case of a relapse.

Our chief recreation, our sole consolation, during the long weeks of our imprisonment, was to watch from our windows the pleasure-seekers passing by in small open boats, and to reflect what an awful day they had had, or were going to have, as the case might be.

In the forenoon they would head up stream – young men with their sweethearts; nephews taking out their rich old aunts; husbands and wives (some of them pairs, some of them odd ones); stylish-looking girls with cousins; energetic-looking men with dogs; high-class silent parties; low-class noisy parties; quarrelsome family parties – boatload after boatload they went by, wet, but still hopeful, pointing out bits of blue sky to each other.

In the evening they would return, drenched and gloomy, saying disagreeable things to one another.

One couple, and one couple only, out of the many hundreds that passed under our review, came back from the ordeal with pleasant faces. He was rowing hard and singing, with a handkerchief tied round his head to keep his hat on, and she was laughing at him, while trying to hold up an umbrella with one hand and steer with the other.

There are but two explanations to account for people being jolly on the river in the rain. The one I dismissed as being both uncharitable and improbable. The other was creditable to the human race, and, adopting it, I took off my cap to this damp but cheerful pair as they went by. They answered with a wave of the hand, and I stood looking after them till they disappeared in the mist.

I am inclined to think that those young people, if they be still alive, are happy. Maybe, fortune has been kind to them, or maybe she has not, but in either event they are, I am inclined to think, happier than are most people.

Now and again, the daily tornado would rage with such fury as to defeat its own purpose by prematurely exhausting itself. On these rare occasions we would sit out on the deck, and enjoy the unwonted luxury of fresh air.

I remember well those few pleasant evenings: the river, luminous with the drowned light, the dark banks where the night lurked, the storm-tossed sky, jewelled here and there with stars.

It was delightful not to hear for an hour or so the sullen threshing of the rain; but to listen to the leaping of the fishes, the soft swirl raised by some water-rat, swimming stealthily among the rushes, the restless twitterings of the few still wakeful birds.

An old corncrake lived near to us, and the way he used to disturb all the other birds, and keep them from going to sleep, was shameful. Amenda, who was town-bred, mistook him at first for one of those cheap alarm clocks, and wondered who was winding him up, and why they went on doing it all night; and, above all, why they didn't oil him.

He would begin his unhallowed performance about dusk, just as every respectable bird was preparing to settle down for the night. A family of thrushes had their nest a few yards from his stand, and they used to get perfectly furious with him.

'There's that fool at it again,' the female thrush would say; 'why can't he do it in the day-time if he must do it at all?' (She spoke, of course, in twitters, but I am confident the above is a correct translation.)

After a while, the young thrushes would wake up and begin chirping, and then the mother would get madder than ever.

'Can't you say something to him?' she would cry indignantly to her husband. 'How do you think the children can get to sleep, poor things, with that hideous row going on all night? Might just as well be living in a saw-mill.'

Thus adjured, the male thrush would put his head over the nest, and call out in a nervous, apologetic manner:–

'I say, you know, you there, I wish you wouldn't mind being quiet a bit. My wife says she can't get the children to sleep. It's too bad, you know, 'pon my word it is.'

'Gor on,' the corncrake would answer surlily. 'You keep your wife herself quiet; that's enough for you to do.' And on he would go again worse than before.

Then a mother blackbird, from a little further off, would join in the fray.

'Ah, it's a good hiding he wants, not a talking to. And if I was a cock, I'd give it him.' (This remark would be made in a tone of withering contempt, and would appear to bear reference to some previous discussion.)

'You're quite right, ma'am,' Mrs Thrush would reply. 'That's what I tell my husband, but' (with rising inflection, so that every lady in the plantation might hear) '*he* wouldn't move himself, bless you – no, not if I and the children were to die before his eyes for want of sleep.'

'Ah, he ain't the only one, my dear,' the blackbird would pipe back, 'they're all alike'; then, in a voice more of sorrow than of anger:– 'but there, it ain't their fault, I suppose, poor things. If you ain't got the spirit of a bird you can't help yourself.'

I would strain my ears at this point to hear if the male blackbird was moved at all by these taunts, but the only sound I could ever detect coming from his neighbourhood was that of palpably exaggerated snoring.

By this time the whole glade would be awake, expressing views concerning that corncrake that would have wounded a less callous nature.

'Blow me tight, Bill,' some vulgar little hedge-sparrow would chirp out, in the midst of the hubbub, 'if I don't believe the gent thinks 'e's a-singing.'

'Tain't 'is fault,' Bill would reply, with mock sympathy. 'Somebody's put a penny in the slot, and 'e can't stop 'isself.'

Irritated by the laugh that this would call forth from the younger birds, the corncrake would exert himself to be more objectionable than ever, and, as a means to this end, would commence giving his marvellous imitation of the sharpening of a rusty saw by a steel file.

But at this an old crow, not to be trifled with, would cry out angrily:–

'Stop that, now. If I come down to you I'll peck your cranky head off, I will.'

And then would follow silence for a quarter of an hour, after which the whole thing would begin again.

CHAPTER V

Brown and MacShaughnassy came down together on the Saturday afternoon; and, as soon as they had dried themselves, and had had some tea, we settled down to work.

Jephson had written that he would not be able to be with us until late in the evening, and Brown proposed that we should occupy ourselves until his arrival with plots.

'Let each of us,' said he, 'sketch out a plot. Afterwards we can compare them, and select the best.'

This we proceeded to do. The plots themselves I forget, but I remember that at the subsequent judging each man selected his own, and became so indignant at the bitter criticism to which it was subjected by the other two, that he tore it up; and, for the next half-hour, we sat and smoked in silence.

When I was very young I yearned to know other people's opinion of me and all my works; now, my chief aim is to avoid hearing it. In those days, had any one told me there was half a line about myself in a newspaper, I should have tramped London to obtain that publication. Now, when I see a column headed with my name, I hurriedly fold up the paper and put it away from me, subduing my natural curiosity to read it by saying to myself, 'Why should you? It will only upset you for the day.'

In my cubhood I possessed a friend. Other friends have come into my life since — very dear and precious friends — but they have none of them been to me quite what this friend was. Because he was my first friend, and we lived together in a world that was much bigger than this world — more full of joy and of grief; and, in that world, we loved and hated deeper than we love and hate in this smaller world that I have come to dwell in since.

He also had the very young man's craving to be criticised, and we made it our custom to oblige each other. We did not know then that what we meant, when we asked for 'criticism,' was encouragement. We thought that we were strong – one does at the beginning of the battle, and that we could bear to hear the truth.

Accordingly, each one pointed out to the other one his errors, and this task kept us both so busy that we had never time to say a word of praise to one another. That we each had a high opinion of the other's talents I am convinced, but our heads were full of silly saws. We said to ourselves: 'There are many who will praise a man; it is only his friend who will tell him of his faults.' Also, we said: 'No man sees his own shortcomings, but when these are pointed out to him by another he is grateful, and proceeds to mend them.'

As we came to know the world better, we learnt the fallacy of these ideas. But then it was too late, for the mischief had been done.

When one of us had written anything, he would read it to the other, and when he had finished he would say, 'Now, tell me what you think of it – frankly and as a friend.'

Those were his words. But his thoughts, though he may not have known them, were:–

'Tell me it is clever and good, my friend, even if you do not think so. The world is very cruel to those that have not yet conquered it, and, though we keep a careless face, our young hearts are scored with wrinkles. Often we grow weary and faint-hearted. Is it not so, my friend? No one has faith in us, and in our dark hours we doubt ourselves. You are my comrade. You know what of myself I have put into this thing that to others will be but an idle half-hour's reading. Tell me it is good, my friend. Put a little heart into me, I pray you.'

But the other, full of the lust of criticism, which is civilisation's substitute for cruelty, would answer more in frankness than in friendship. Then he who had written would flush angrily, and scornful words would pass.

One evening, he read me a play he had written. There was much that was good in it, but there were also faults (there are in some plays), and these I seized upon and made merry over. I could hardly have dealt out to the piece more unnecessary bitterness had I been a professional critic.

As soon as I paused from my sport he rose, and, taking his manuscript from the table, tore it in two, and flung it in the fire – he was but a very young man, you must remember – and then, standing before me with a white face, told, me, unsolicited, his opinion of me and of my art. After which double event, it is perhaps needless to say that we parted in hot anger.

I did not see him again for years. The streets of life are very crowded, and if we loose each other's hands we are soon hustled far apart. When I did next meet him it was by accident.

I had left the Whitehall Rooms after a public dinner, and, glad of the cool night air, was strolling home by the Embankment. A man, slouching along under the trees, paused as I overtook him.

'You couldn't oblige me with a light, could you, guv'nor?' he said. The voice sounded strange, coming from the figure that it did.

I struck a match, and held it out to him, shaded by my hands. As the faint light illumined his face, I started back, and let the match fall:–

'Harry!'

He answered with a short dry laugh. 'I didn't know it was you,' he said, 'or I shouldn't have stopped you.'

'How has it come to this, old fellow?' I asked, laying my hand upon his shoulder. His coat was unpleasantly greasy, and I drew my hand away again as quickly as I could, and tried to wipe it covertly upon my handkerchief.

'Oh, it's a long story,' he answered carelessly, 'and too

conventional to be worth telling. Some of us go up, you know.
Some of us go down. You're doing pretty well, I hear.'

'I suppose so,' I replied; 'I've climbed a few feet up a greasy
pole, and am trying to stick there. But it is of you I want to
talk. Can't I do anything for you?'

We were passing under a gas-lamp at the moment. He thrust
his face forward close to mine, and the light fell full and
pitilessly upon it.

'Do I look like a man you could do anything for?' he said.

We walked on in silence side by side, I casting about for
words that might seize hold of him.

'You needn't worry about me,' he continued after a while,
'I'm comfortable enough. We take life easily down here where I
am. We've no disappointments.'

'Why did you give up like a weak coward?' I burst out
angrily. 'You had talent. You would have won with ordinary
perseverance.'

'Maybe,' he replied, in the same even tone of indifference. 'I
suppose I hadn't the grit. I think if somebody had believed in
me it might have helped me. But nobody did, and at last I lost
belief in myself. And when a man loses that, he's like a balloon
with the gas let out.'

I listened to his words in indignation and astonishment.
'Nobody believed in you!' I repeated. 'Why, *I* always believed
in you, you know that. I ——'

Then I paused, remembering our 'candid criticism' of one
another.

'Did you?' he replied quietly, 'I never heard you say so.
Good-night.'

In the course of our Strandward walking we had come to the
neighbourhood of the Savoy, and, as he spoke, he disappeared
down one of the dark turnings thereabouts.

I hastened after him, calling him by name, but though I
heard his quick steps before me for a little way, they were soon
swallowed up in the sound of other steps, and, when I reached

the square in which the chapel stands, I had lost all trace of him.

A policeman was standing by the churchyard railings, and of him I made inquiries.

'What sort of a gent was he, sir?' questioned the man.

'A tall, thin gentleman, very shabbily dressed – might be mistaken for a tramp.'

'Ah, there's a good many of that sort living in this town,' replied the man. 'I'm afraid you'll have some difficulty in finding him.'

Thus for a second time had I heard his footsteps die away, knowing I should never listen for their drawing near again.

I wondered as I walked on – I have wondered before and since – whether Art, even with a capital A, is quite worth all the suffering that is inflicted in her behalf – whether she and we are better for all the scorning and the sneering, all the envying and the hating, that is done in her name.

Jephson arrived about nine o'clock in the ferry-boat. We were made acquainted with this fact by having our heads bumped against the sides of the saloon.

Somebody or other always had their head bumped whenever the ferry-boat arrived. It was a heavy and cumbersome machine, and the ferry-boy was not a good punter. He admitted this frankly, which was creditable of him. But he made no attempt to improve himself; that is, where he was wrong. His method was to arrange the punt before starting in a line with the point towards which he wished to proceed, and then to push hard, without ever looking behind him, until something suddenly stopped him. This was sometimes the bank, sometimes another boat, occasionally a steamer, from six to a dozen times a day our riparian dwelling. That he never succeeded in staving the houseboat in speaks highly for the man who built her.

One day he came down upon us with a tremendous crash.

Amenda was walking along the passage at the moment, and the result to her was that she received a violent blow first on the left side of her head and then on the right.

She was accustomed to accept one bump as a matter of course, and to regard it as an intimation from the boy that he had come; but this double knock annoyed her: so much 'style' was out of place in a mere ferry-boy. Accordingly she went out to him in a state of high indignation.

Boxed his ears

'What do you think you are?' she cried, balancing accounts by boxing his ears first on one side and then on the other, 'a torpedo! What are you doing here at all? What do you want?'

'I don't want nothin',' explained the boy, rubbing his head; 'I've brought a gent down.'

'A gent?' said Amenda, looking round, but seeing no one. 'What gent?'

'A stout gent in a straw 'at,' answered the boy, staring round him bewilderedly.

'Well, where is he?' asked Amenda.

'I dunno,' replied the boy, in an awed voice; ''e was a-standin' there, at the other end of the punt, a-smokin' a cigar.'

Just then a head appeared above the water, and a spent but infuriated swimmer struggled up between the houseboat and the bank.

'Oh, there 'e is!' cried the boy delightedly, evidently much relieved at this satisfactory solution of the mystery; ''e must ha' tumbled off the punt.'

'You're quite right, my lad, that's just what he did do, and there's your fee for assisting him to do it.' Saying which, my dripping friend, who had now scrambled upon deck, leant over, and following Amenda's excellent example, expressed his feelings upon the boy's head.

There was one comforting reflection about the transaction as a whole, and that was that the ferry-boy had at last received a fit and proper reward for his services. I had often felt inclined to give him something myself. I think he was, without exception, the most clumsy and stupid boy I have ever come across; and that is saying a good deal.

His mother undertook that for three-and-sixpence a week he should 'make himself generally useful' to us for a couple of hours every morning.

Those were the old lady's very words, and I repeated them to Amenda when I introduced the boy to her.

'This is James, Amenda,' I said; 'he will come down here every morning at seven, and bring us our milk and the letters, and from then till nine he will make himself generally useful.'

Amenda took stock of him.

'It will be a change of occupation for him, sir, I should say, by the look of him,' she remarked.

After that, whenever some more than usually stirring crash or blood-curdling bump would cause us to leap from our seats and cry: 'What on earth has happened?' Amenda would reply: 'Oh, it's only James, mum, making himself generally useful.'

Whatever he lifted he let fall; whatever he touched he upset; whatever he came near – that was not a fixture – he knocked over; if it was a fixture, it knocked *him* over. This was not carelessness: it seemed to be a natural gift. Never in his life, I am convinced, had he carried a bucketful of anything any-where without tumbling over it before he got there. One of his duties was to water the flowers on the roof. Fortunately – for the flowers – Nature, that summer, stood drinks with a lavishness sufficient to satisfy the most confirmed vegetable toper: otherwise every plant on our boat would have died from drought. Never one drop of water did they receive from him. He was for ever taking them water, but he never arrived there with it. As a rule he upset the pail before he got it on to the boat at all, and this was the best thing that could happen, because then the water simply went back into the river, and did no harm to any one. Sometimes, however, he would succeed in landing it, and then the chances were he would spill it over the deck or into the passage. Now and again, he would get halfway up the ladder before the accident occurred. Twice he nearly reached the top; and once he actually did gain the roof. What happened there on that memorable occasion will never be known. The boy himself, when picked up, could explain nothing. It is supposed that he lost his head with the pride of the achievement, and essayed feats that neither his previous training nor his natural abilities justified him in attempting. However that may be, the fact remains that the main body of the water came down the kitchen chimney; and that the boy and the empty pail arrived together on deck before they knew they had started.

When he could find nothing else to damage, he would go out of his way to upset himself. He could not be sure of stepping from his own punt on to the boat with safety. As often as not, he would catch his foot in the chain or the punt-pole, and arrive on his chest.

Amenda used to condole with him. 'Your mother ought to be ashamed of herself,' I heard her telling him one morning; 'she could never have taught you to walk. What you want is a go-cart.'

He was a willing lad, but his stupidity was supernatural. A comet appeared in the sky that year, and everybody was talking about it. One day he said to me:—

'There's a comet coming, ain't there, sir?' He talked about it as though it were a circus.

'Coming!' I answered, 'it's come. Haven't you seen it?'

'No, sir.'

'Oh, well, you have a look for it to-night. It's worth seeing.'

'Yees, sir, I should like to see it. It's got a tail, ain't it, sir?'

'Yes, a very fine tail.'

'Yees, sir, they said it 'ad a tail. Where do you go to see it, sir?'

'Go! You don't want to go anywhere. You'll see it in your own garden at ten o'clock.'

He thanked me, and, tumbling over a sack of potatoes, plunged head foremost into his punt and departed.

Next morning, I asked him if he had seen the comet.

'No, sir, I couldn't see it anywhere.'

'Did you look?'

'Yees, sir. I looked a long time.'

'How on earth did you manage to miss it then?' I exclaimed. 'It was a clear enough night. Where did you look?'

'In our garden, sir. Where you told me.'

'Whereabouts in the garden?' chimed in Amenda, who happened to be standing by; 'under the gooseberry bushes?'

'Yees – everywhere.'

That is what he had done: he had taken the stable lantern and searched the garden for it.

But the day when he broke even his own record for foolishness happened about three weeks later. MacShaughnassy was staying with us at the time, and on the Friday evening he mixed us a salad, according to a recipe given him by his aunt. On the Saturday morning, everybody was, of course, very ill. Everybody always is very ill after partaking of any dish prepared by MacShaughnassy. Some people attempt to explain this fact by talking glibly of 'cause and effect.' MacShaughnassy maintains that it is simply coincidence.

'How do you know,' he says, 'that you wouldn't have been ill if you hadn't eaten any? You're queer enough now, any one can see, and I'm very sorry for you; but, for all that you can tell, if you hadn't eaten any of that stuff you might have been very much worse – perhaps dead. In all probability, it has saved your life.' And for the rest of the day, he assumes towards you the attitude of a man who has dragged you from the grave.

The moment Jimmy arrived I seized hold of him.

'Jimmy,' I said, 'you must rush off to the chemist's immediately. Don't stop for anything. Tell him to give you something for colic – the result of vegetable poisoning. It must be something very strong, and enough for four. Don't forget, something to counteract the effects of vegetable poisoning. Hurry up, or it may be too late.'

My excitement communicated itself to the boy. He tumbled back into his punt, and pushed off vigorously. I watched him land, and disappear in the direction of the village.

Half an hour passed, but Jimmy did not return. No one felt sufficiently energetic to go after him. We had only just strength enough to sit still and feebly abuse him. At the end of an hour we were all feeling very much better. At the end of an hour and a half we were glad he had not returned when he ought to have, and were only curious as to what had become of him.

In the evening, strolling through the village, we saw him sitting by the open door of his mother's cottage, with a shawl wrapped round him. He was looking worn and ill.

'Why, Jimmy,' I said, 'what's the matter? Why didn't you come back this morning?'

'I couldn't, sir,' Jimmy answered, 'I was so queer. Mother made me go to bed.'

'You seemed all right in the morning,' I said; 'what's made you queer?'

'What Mr Jones give me, sir: it upset me awful.'

A light broke in upon me.

'What did you say, Jimmy, when you got to Mr Jones's shop?' I asked.

'I told 'im what you said, sir, that 'e was to give me something to counteract the effects of vegetable poisoning. And that it was to be very strong, and enough for four.'

He was looking worn and ill

'And what did he say?'

''E said that was only your nonsense, sir, and that I'd better have enough for one to begin with; and then 'e asked me if I'd been eating green apples again.'

'And you told him?'

'Yees, sir, I told 'im I'd 'ad a few, and 'e said it served me right, and that 'e 'oped it would be a warning to me. And then 'e put something fizzy in a glass and told me to drink it.'

'And you drank it?'

'Yees, sir.'

'It never occurred to you, Jimmy, that there was nothing the matter with you – that you were never feeling better in your life, and that you did not require any medicine?'

'No, sir.'

'Did one single scintilla of thought of any kind occur to you in connection with the matter, Jimmy, from beginning to end?'

'No, sir.'

People who never met Jimmy disbelieve this story. They argue that its premises are in disaccord with the known laws governing human nature, that its details do not square with the average of probability. People who have seen and conversed with Jimmy accept it with simple faith.

The advent of Jephson – which I trust the reader has not entirely forgotten – cheered us up considerably. Jephson was always at his best when all other things were at their worst. It was not that he struggled in Mark Tapley fashion to appear most cheerful when most depressed; it was that petty misfortunes and mishaps genuinely amused and inspirited him. Most of us can recall our unpleasant experiences with amused affection; Jephson possessed the robuster philosophy that enabled him to enjoy his during their actual progress. He arrived drenched to the skin, chuckling hugely at the idea of having come down on a visit to a houseboat in such weather.

Under his warming influence, the hard lines on our faces thawed, and by supper time we were, as all Englishmen and women who wish to enjoy life should be, independent of the weather.

Later on, as if disheartened by our indifference, the rain ceased, and we took our chairs out on the deck, and sat watching the lightning, which still played incessantly. Then, not unnaturally, the talk drifted into a sombre channel, and we began recounting stories, dealing with the gloomy and mysterious side of life.

Some of these were worth remembering, and some were not. The one that left the strongest impression on my mind was a tale that Jephson told us.

I had been relating a somewhat curious experience of my own. I met a man in the Strand one day that I knew very well, as I thought, though I had not seen him for years. We walked together to Charing Cross, and there we shook hands and parted. Next morning, I spoke of this meeting to a mutual friend, and then I learnt, for the first time, that the man had died six months before.

The natural inference was that I had mistaken one man for another, an error that, not having a good memory for faces, I frequently fall into. What was remarkable about the matter, however, was that throughout our walk I had conversed with the man under the impression that he was that other dead man, and, whether by coincidence or not, his replies had never once suggested to me my mistake.

As soon as I had finished, Jephson, who had been listening very thoughtfully, asked me if I believed in spiritualism 'to its fullest extent.'

'That is rather a large question,' I answered. 'What do you mean by "spiritualism to its fullest extent"?'

'Well, do you believe that the spirits of the dead have not only the power of revisiting this earth at their will,

We walked together to Charing Cross

but that, when here, they have the power of action, or rather, of exciting to action? Let me put a definite case. A spiritualist friend of mine, a sensible and by no means imaginative man, once told me that a table, through the medium of which the spirit of a friend had been in the habit of communicating with him, came slowly across the room towards him, of its own accord, one night as he sat alone, and pinioned him against the wall. Now can any of you believe that, or can't you?'

'I could,' Brown took it upon himself to reply; 'but, before doing so, I should wish for an introduction to the friend who told you the story. Speaking generally,' he continued, 'it seems to me that the difference between what we call the natural and the supernatural is merely the difference between frequency and rarity of occurrence. Having regard to the phenomena we are compelled to admit, I think it illogical to disbelieve anything we are unable to disprove.'

'For my part,' remarked MacShaughnassy, 'I can believe in the ability of our spirit friends to give the quaint entertainments credited to them much easier than I can in their desire to do so.'

'You mean,' added Jephson, 'that you cannot understand why a spirit, not compelled as we are by the exigencies of society, should care to spend its evenings carrying on a laboured and childish conversation with a room full of abnormally uninteresting people.'

'That is precisely what I cannot understand,' MacShaughnassy agreed.

'Nor I, either,' said Jephson. 'But I was thinking of something very different altogether. Suppose a man died with the dearest wish of his heart unfulfilled, do you believe that his spirit might have power to return to earth and complete the interrupted work?'

'Well,' answered MacShaughnassy, 'if one admits the possibility of spirits retaining any interest in the affairs of this world at all, it is certainly more reasonable to imagine them engaged upon a task such as you suggest, than to believe that they occupy themselves with the performance of mere drawing-room tricks. But what are you leading up to?'

'Why, to this,' replied Jephson, seating himself straddle-legged across his chair, and leaning his arms upon the back. 'I was told a story this morning at the hospital by an old French doctor. The actual facts are few and simple; all that is known can be read in the Paris police records of sixty-two years ago.

'The most important part of the case, however, is the part that is not know, and that never will be known.

'The story begins with a great wrong done by one man unto another man. What the wrong was I do not know. I am inclined to think, however, it was connected with a woman. I think that, because he who had been wronged hated him who had wronged him with a hate such as does not often burn in a man's brain, unless it be fanned by the memory of a woman's breath.

'Still that is only conjecture, and the point is immaterial. The man who had done the wrong fled, and the other man followed him. It became a point-to-point race, the first man having the advantage of a day's start. The course was the whole world, and the stakes were the first man's life.

'Travellers were few and far between in those days, and this made the trail easy to follow. The first man, never knowing how far or how near the other was behind him, and hoping now and again that he might have baffled him, would rest for a while. The second man, knowing always just how far the first one was before him, never paused, and thus each day the man who was spurred by Hate drew nearer to the man who was spurred by Fear.

'At this town the answer to the never-varied question would be:–

'"At seven o'clock last evening, M'sieur."

'"Seven – ah; eighteen hours. Give me something to eat, quick, while the horses are being put to."

'At the next the calculation would be sixteen hours.

'Passing a lonely châlet, Monsieur puts his head out of the window:—

'"How long since a carriage passed this way, with a tall, fair man inside?"

'"Such a one passed early this morning, M'sieur."

'"Thanks, drive on, a hundred francs apiece if you are through the pass before daybreak."

'Monsieur puts his head out of the window'

'"And what for dead horses, M'sieur?"

'"Twice their value when living."

'One day the man who was ridden by Fear looked up, and saw before him the open door of a cathedral, and, passing in, knelt down and prayed. He prayed long and fervently, for men, when they are in sore straits, clutch eagerly at the straws of faith. He prayed that he might be forgiven his sin, and, more important still, that he might be pardoned the consequences of his sin, and be delivered from his adversary; and a few chairs from him, facing him, knelt his enemy, praying also.

'But the second man's prayer, being a thanksgiving merely, was short, so that when the first man raised his eyes, he saw the face of his enemy gazing at him across the chair-tops, with a mocking smile upon it.

'He made no attempt to rise, but remained kneeling, fascinated by the look of joy that shone out of the other man's eyes. And the other man moved the high-backed chairs one by one, and came towards him softly.

'Then, just as the man who had been wronged stood beside the man who had wronged him, full of gladness that his opportunity had come, there burst from the cathedral tower a sudden clash of bells, and the man, whose opportunity had come, broke his heart and fell back dead, with that mocking smile still playing round his mouth.

'And so he lay there.

'Then the man who had done the wrong rose up and passed out, praising God.

'What became of the body of the other man is not known. It was the body of a stranger who had died suddenly in the cathedral. There was none to identify it, none to claim it.

'Years passed away, and the survivor in the tragedy became a worthy and useful citizen, and a noted man of science.

'In his laboratory were many objects necessary to him in his researches, and, prominent among them, stood in a certain corner a human skeleton. It was a very old and much-mended skeleton, and one day the long-expected end arrived, and it tumbled to pieces.

'Thus it became necessary to purchase another.

'The man of science visited a dealer he well knew – a little parchment-faced old man who kept a dingy shop, where nothing was ever sold, within the shadow of the towers of Notre Dame.

'The little parchment-faced old man had just the very thing that Monsieur wanted – a singularly fine and well-proportioned "study". It should be sent round and set up in Monsieur's laboratory that very afternoon.

'The dealer was as good as his word. When Monsieur entered his laboratory that evening, the thing was in its place.

'Monsieur seated himself in his high-backed chair, and tried to collect his thoughts. But Monsieur's thoughts were unruly, and inclined to wander, and to wander always in one direction.

'Monsieur opened a large volume and commenced to read. He read of a man who had wronged another and fled from him, the other man following. Finding himself reading this, he closed the book angrily, and went and stood by the window and looked out. He saw before him the sun-pierced nave of a great cathedral, and on the stones lay a dead man with a mocking smile upon his face.

'Cursing himself for a fool, he turned away with a laugh. But his laugh was short-lived, for it seemed to him that something else in the room was laughing also. Struck suddenly still, with his feet glued to the ground, he stood listening for a while: then sought with starting eyes the corner from where the sound had seemed to come. But the white thing standing there was only grinning.

'Monsieur wiped the damp sweat from his head and hands, and stole out.

'For a couple of days he did not enter the room again. On the third, telling himself that his fears were those of a hysterical girl, he opened the door and went in. To shame himself, he took his lamp in his hand, and crossing over to the far corner where the skeleton stood, examined it. A set of bones bought for three hundred francs. Was he a child, to be scared by such a bogey!

'He held his lamp up in front of the thing's grinning head. The flame of the lamp flickered as though a faint breath had passed over it.

'The man explained this to himself by saying that the walls of the house were old and cracked, and that the wind might creep in anywhere. He repeated this explanation to himself as he recrossed the room, walking backwards, with his eyes fixed on the thing. When he reached his desk, he sat down and gripped the arms of his chair till his fingers turned white.

'He tried to work, but the empty sockets in that grinning head seemed to be drawing him towards them. He rose and battled with his inclination to fly screaming from the room. Glancing fearfully about him, his eye fell upon a high screen, standing before the door. He dragged it forward, and placed it between himself and the thing, so that he could not see it – nor it see him. Then he sat down again to his work. For a while he forced himself to look at the book in front of him, but at last, unable to control himself any longer, he suffered his eyes to follow their own bent.

'It may have been an hallucination. He may have accidentally placed the screen so as to favour such an illusion. But what he saw was a bony hand coming round the corner of the screen, and, with a cry, he fell to the floor in a swoon.

'The people of the house came running in, and lifting him up, carried him out, and laid him upon his bed. As soon as he recovered, his first question was, where had they found the thing – where was it when they entered the room? and when they told him they had seen it standing where it always stood, and had gone down into the room to look again, because of his frenzied entreaties, and returned trying to hide their smiles, he listened to their talk about overwork, and the necessity for change and rest, and said they might do with him as they would.

'So for many months the laboratory door remained locked. Then there came a chill autumn evening when the man of science opened it again, and closed it behind him.

'He lighted his lamp, and gathered his instruments and books around him, and sat down before them in his high-backed chair. And the old terror returned to him.

'But this time he meant to conquer himself. His nerves were stronger now, and his brain clearer; he would fight his unreasoning fear. He crossed to the door and locked himself in, and flung the key to the other end of the room, where it fell among jars and bottles with an echoing clatter.

'Later on, his old housekeeper, going her final round, tapped at his door and wished him good-night, as was her custom. She received no response, at first, and, growing nervous, tapped louder and called again; and at length an answering "good-night" came back to her.

'She thought little about it at the time, but afterwards she remembered that the voice that had replied to her had been strangely grating and mechanical. Trying to describe it, she likened it to such a voice as she would imagine coming from a statue.

'Next morning his door remained still locked. It was no unusual thing for him to work all night and far into the next day, so no one thought to be surprised. When, however, evening came, and yet he did not appear, his servants gathered outside the room and whispered, remembering what had happened once before.

'They listened, but could hear no sound. They shook the door and called to him, then beat with their fists upon the wooden panels. But still no sound came from the room.

'Becoming alarmed, they decided to burst open the door, and, after many blows, it gave way, and they crowded in.

'He sat bolt upright in his high-backed chair. They thought at first he had died in his sleep. But when they drew nearer and the light fell upon him, they saw the livid marks of bony fingers round his throat; and in his eyes there was a terror such as is not often seen in human eyes.'

Brown was the first to break the silence that followed. He asked me if I had any brandy on board. He said he felt he should like just a nip of brandy before going to bed. That is one of the chief charms of Jephson's stories: they always make you feel you want a little brandy.

CHAPTER VI

'Cats', remarked Jephson to me, one afternoon, as we sat in the punt discussing the plot of our novel, 'cats are animals for whom I entertain a very great respect. Cats and Nonconformists seem to me the only things in this world possessed of a practicable working conscience. Watch a cat doing something mean and wrong – if ever one gives you the chance; notice how anxious she is that nobody should see her doing it; and how prompt, if detected, to pretend that she was not doing it – that she was not even thinking of doing it – that, as a matter of fact, she was just about to do something else, quite different. You might almost think they had a soul.

'Only this morning I was watching that tortoiseshell of yours on the houseboat. She was creeping along the roof, behind the flower-boxes, stalking a young thrush that had perched upon a coil of rope. Murder gleamed from her eye, assassination lurked in every twitching muscle of her body. As she crouched to spring, Fate, for once favouring the weak, directed her attention to myself, and she became, for the first time, aware of my presence. It acted upon her as a heavenly vision upon a Biblical criminal. In an instant she was a changed being. The wicked beast, going about seeking whom it might devour, had vanished. In its place sat a long-tailed, furry angel, gazing up into the sky with an expression that was one-third innocence and two-thirds admiration of the beauties of nature. What was she doing there, did I want to know? Why, could I not see, playing with a bit of earth. Surely I was not so evil-minded as to imagine she wanted to kill that dear little bird – God bless it.

'Then note an old Tom, slinking home in the early morning, after a night spent on a roof of bad repute. Can you picture to yourself a living creature less eager to attract attention? "Dear me," you can all but hear it saying to itself, "I'd no idea it was so late; how time does go when one is enjoying oneself. I do hope I shan't meet any one I know – very awkward, it's being so light."

'In the distance it sees a policeman, and stops suddenly within the shelter of a shadow. "Now what's he doing there," it says, "and close to our door too? I can't go in while he's hanging about. He's sure to see and recognise me; and he's just the sort of man to talk to the servants."

'It hides itself behind a post and waits, peeping cautiously round the corner from time to time. The policeman, however, seems to have taken up his residence at that particular spot, and the cat becomes worried and excited.

'"What's the matter with the fool?" it mutters indignantly; "is he dead? Why don't he move on, he's always telling other people to. Stupid ass."

'Just then a far-off cry of "milk" is heard, and the cat starts up in an agony of alarm. "Great Scott, hark at that! Why, everybody will be down before I get in. Well, I can't help it. I must chance it."

'He glances round at himself, and hesitates. "I wouldn't mind if I didn't look so dirty and untidy," he muses; "people are so prone to think evil in this world."

"Ah, well," he adds, giving himself a shake, "there's nothing else for it, I must put my trust in Providence, it's pulled me through before: here goes."

'He assumes an aspect of chastened sorrow, and trots along with a demure and saddened step. It is evident he wishes to convey the idea that he has been out all night on work connected with the Vigilance Association, and is now returning home sick at heart because of the sights that he has seen.

'He squirms in, unnoticed, through a window, and has just time to give himself a hurried lick down before he hears the cook's step on the stairs. When she enters the kitchen he is curled up on the hearth-rug, fast asleep. The opening of the shutters awakes him. He rises and comes forward, yawning and stretching himself.

"Dear me, is it morning then?" he says drowsily. "Heigh-ho! I've had such a lovely sleep, cook; and such a beautiful dream about poor mother."

'Cats! do you call them? Why, they are Christians in everything except the number of legs.'

'They certainly are,' I responded, 'wonderfully cunning little animals, and it is not by their moral and religious instincts alone that they are so closely linked to man; the marvellous ability they display in taking care of "number one" is worthy of the human race itself. Some friends of mine had a cat, a big black Tom: they have got half of him still. They had reared him from a kitten, and, in their homely, undemonstrative way, they liked him. There was nothing, however, approaching passion on either side.

'One day a Chinchilla came to live in the neighbourhood, under the charge of an elderly spinster, and the two cats met at a garden wall party.

'"What sort of diggings have you got?" asked the Chinchilla.

'"Oh, pretty fair."

'"Nice people?"

'"Yes, nice enough – as people go."

'"Pretty willing? Look after you well, and all that sort of thing?"

'"Yes – oh yes. I've no fault to find with them."

'"What's the victuals like?"

'"Oh, the usual thing, you know, bones and scraps, and a bit of dog-biscuit now and then for a change."

'"Bones and dog-biscuits! Do you mean to say you eat bones?"

'"Yes, when I can get 'em. Why what's wrong about them?"

'"Shade of Egyptian Isis, bones and dog-biscuits! Don't you ever get any spring chickens, or a sardine, or a lamb cutlet?"

'"Chickens! Sardines! What are you talking about? What are sardines?"

"'What are sardines! Oh, my dear child (the Chinchilla was a lady cat, and always called the gentlemen friends a little older than herself, "dear child"), these people of yours are treating you just shamefully. Come, sit down and tell me all about it. What do they give you to sleep on?"

"'The floor."

"'I thought so; and skim milk and water to drink, I suppose?"

"'It *is* a bit thin."

"'I can quite imagine it. You must leave these people, my dear, at once."

"'But where am I to go to?"

"'Anywhere."

"'But who'll take me in?"

"'Anybody, if you go the right way to work. How many times do you think I've changed my people? Seven! – and bettered myself on each occasion. Why, do you know where I was born? In a pig-sty. There were three of us, mother and I and my little brother. Mother would leave us every evening, returning generally just as it was getting light. One morning she did not come back. We waited and waited, but the day passed on and she did not return, and we grew hungrier and hungrier, and at last we lay down, side by side, and cried ourselves to sleep.

"'In the evening, peeping through a hole in the door, we saw her coming across the field. She was crawling very slowly, with her body close down against the ground. We called to her, and she answered with a low 'crroo'; but she did not hasten her pace.

"'She crept in and rolled over on her side, and we ran to her, for we were almost starving. We lay long upon her breasts, and she licked us over and over.

"'I dropped asleep upon her, and in the night I awoke, feeling cold. I crept closer to her, but that only made me colder still, and she was wet and clammy with a dark moisture that was oozing from her side. I did not know what it was at that time, but I have learnt since.

'"That was when I could hardly have been four weeks old, and from that day to this I've looked after myself: you've got to do that in this world, my dear. For a while, I and my brother lived on in that sty and kept ourselves. It was a grim struggle at first, two babies fighting for life; but we pulled through. At the end of about three months, wandering farther from home than usual, I came upon a cottage, standing in the fields. It looked warm and cosy through the open door, and I went in: I have always been blessed with plenty of nerve. Some children were playing round the fire, and they welcomed me and made much of me. It was a new sensation to me, and I stayed there. I thought the place a palace at the time.

'"I might have gone on thinking so if it had not been that, passing through the village one day, I happened to catch sight of a room behind a shop. There was a carpet on the floor, and a rug before the fire. I had never known till then that there were such luxuries in the world. I determined to make that shop my home, and I did so."

'"How did you manage it?" asked the black cat, who was growing interested.

'"By the simple process of walking in and sitting down. My dear child, cheek's the 'Open sesame' to every door. The cat that works hard dies of starvation, the cat that has brains is kicked downstairs for a fool, and the cat that has virtue is drowned for a scamp; but the cat that has cheek sleeps on a velvet cushion and dines on cream and horseflesh. I marched straight in and rubbed myself against the old man's legs. He and his wife were quite taken with what they called my 'trustfulness,' and adopted me with enthusiasm. Strolling about the fields of an evening I often used to hear the children of the cottage calling my name. It was weeks before they gave up seeking for me. One of them, the youngest, would sob herself to sleep of a night, thinking that I was dead: they were affectionate children.

"'I boarded with my shopkeeping friends for nearly a year, and from them I went to some new people who had lately come to the neighbourhood, and who possessed a really excellent cook. I think I could have been very satisfied with these people, but, unfortunately, they came down in the world, and had to give up the big house and the cook, and take a cottage, and I did not care to go back to that sort of life.

"'Accordingly I looked about for a fresh opening. There was a curious old fellow who lived not far off. People said he was rich, but nobody liked him. He was shaped differently from other men. I turned the matter over in my mind for a day or two, and then determined to give him a trial. Being a lonely sort of man, he might make a fuss over me, and if not I could go.

"'My surmise proved correct. I have never been more petted than I was by 'Toady,' as the village boys had dubbed him. My present guardian is foolish enough over me, goodness knows, but she has other ties, while 'Toady' had nothing else to love, not even himself. He could hardly believe his eyes at first when I jumped up on his knees and rubbed myself against his ugly face. 'Why, Kitty,' he said, 'do you know you're the first living thing that has ever come to me of its own acord.' There were tears in his funny little red eyes as he said that.

"'I remained two years with 'Toady,' and was very happy indeed. Then he fell ill, and strange people came to the house, and I was neglected. 'Toady' liked me to come up and lie upon the bed, where he could stroke me with his long, thin hand, and at first I used to do this. But a sick man is not the best of company, as you can imagine, and the atmosphere of a sick room not too healthy, so, all things considered, I felt it was time for me to make a fresh move.

"'I had some difficulty in getting away. 'Toady' was always asking for me, and they tried to keep me with him: he seemed to lie easier when I was there. I succeeded at length, however, and, once outside the door, I put sufficient distance between myself and the house to ensure my not being captured, for I knew 'Toady' so long as he lived would never cease hoping to get me back.

"'Where to go, I did not know. Two or three homes were offered me, but none of them quite suited me. At one place, where I put up for a day, just to see how I liked it, there was a dog; and at another, which would otherwise have done admirably, they kept a baby. Whatever you do, never stop at a house where they keep a baby. If a child pulls your tail or ties a paper bag round your head, you can give it one for itself and nobody blames you. 'Well, serve you right,' they say to the yelling brat, 'you shouldn't tease the poor thing.' But if you resent a baby's holding you by the throat and trying to gouge out your eye with a wooden ladle, you are called a spiteful beast, and 'shoo'd' all round the garden. If people keep babies, they don't keep me; that's my rule.

"'After sampling some three or four families, I finally fixed upon a banker. Offers more advantageous from a worldly point of view were open to me. I could have gone to a public-house, where the victuals were simply unlimited, and where the back door was left open all night. But about the banker's (he was also a churchwarden, and his wife never smiled at anything less than a joke by the bishop) there was an atmosphere of solid respectability that I felt would be comforting to my nature. My dear child, you will come across cynics who will sneer at respectability: don't you listen to them. Respectability is its own reward – and a very real and practical reward. It may not bring you dainty dishes and soft beds, but it brings you something better and more lasting. It brings you the consciousness that you are living the right life, that you are doing the right thing, that, so far as earthly ingenuity can fix it, you are going to the right place, and that other folks ain't. Don't you ever let any one set you against respectability. It's the most satisfying thing I know of in this world – and about the cheapest.

'"I was nearly three years with this family, and was sorry when I had to go. I should never have left if I could have helped it, but one day something happened at the bank which necessitated the banker's taking a sudden journey to Spain, and, after that, the house became a somewhat unpleasant place to live in. Noisy, disagreeable people were continually knocking at the door and making rows in the passage; and at night folks threw bricks at the windows.

'"I was in a delicate state of health at the time, and my nerves

could not stand it. I said good-bye to the town, and making my way back into the country, put up with a county family.

"'They were great swells, but I should have preferred them had they been more homely. I am of an affectionate disposition, and I like every one about me to love me. They were good enough to me in their distant way, but they did not take much notice of me, and I soon got tired of lavishing attentions on people that neither valued nor responded to them.

"'From these people I went to a retired potato merchant. It was a social descent, but a rise so far as comfort and appreciation were concerned. They appeared to be an exceedingly nice family, and to be extremely fond of me. I say they 'appeared' to be these things, because the sequel proved that they were neither. Six months after I had come to them they went away and left me. They never asked me to accompany them. They made no arrangements for me to stay behind. They evidently did not care what became of me. Such egotistical indifference to the claims of friendship I had never before met with. It shook my faith – never too robust – in human nature. I determined that, in future, no one should have the opportunity of disappointing my trust in them. I selected my present mistress on the recommendation of a gentleman friend of mine who had formerly lived with her. He said she was an excellent caterer. The only reason he had left her was that she expected him to be in at ten each night, and that hour didn't fit in with his other arrangements. It made no difference to me – as a matter of fact, I do not care for these midnight *réunions* that are so popular amongst us. There are always too many cats for one properly to enjoy oneself, and sooner or later a rowdy element is sure to creep in. I offered myself to her, and she accepted me gratefully. But I have never liked her, and never shall. She is a silly old woman, and bores me. She is, however, devoted to me, and, unless something extra attractive turns up, I shall stick to her.

"'That, my dear, is the story of my life, so far as it has gone.

I tell it you to show you how easy it is to be 'taken in.' Fix on your house, and mew piteously at the back door. When it is opened run in and rub yourself against the first leg you come across. Rub hard, and look up confidingly. Nothing gets round  human beings, I have noticed, quicker than confidence. They don't get much of it, and it pleases them. Always be confiding. At the same time be prepared for emergencies. If you are still doubtful as to your reception, try and get yourself slightly wet. Why people should prefer a wet cat to a dry one I have never been able to understand; but that a wet cat is practically sure of being taken in and gushed over, while a dry cat is liable to have the garden hose turned upon it, is an undoubted fact. Also, if you can possibly manage it, and it is offered you, eat a bit of dry bread. The Human Race is always stirred to its deepest depths by the sight of a cat eating a bit of dry bread."

'My friend's black Tom profited by the Chinchilla's wisdom. A catless couple had lately come to live next door. He determined to adopt them on trial. Accordingly, on the first rainy day, he went out soon after lunch and sat for four hours in an open field. In the evening, soaked to the skin, and feeling pretty hungry, he went mewing to their door. One of the maids opened it, he rushed under her skirts and rubbed himself against

her legs. She screamed, and down came the master and the mistress to know what was the matter.

"'It's a stray cat, mum," said the girl.

"'Turn it out," said the master.

"'Oh no, don't," said the mistress.

"'Oh, poor thing, it's wet," said the housemaid.

"'Perhaps it's hungry," said the cook.

"'Try it with a bit of dry bread," sneered the master, who wrote for the newspapers, and thought he knew everything.

'A stale crust was proffered. The cat ate it greedily, and afterwards rubbed himself gratefully against the man's light trousers.

'This made the man ashamed of himself, likewise of his trousers. "Oh, well, let it stop if it wants to," he said.

'So the cat was made comfortable, and stayed on.

'Meanwhile its own family were seeking for it high and low. They had not cared over much for it while they had had it; now it was gone, they were inconsolable. In the light of its absence, it appeared to them the one thing that had made the place home. The shadows of suspicion gathered round the case. The cat's disappearance, at first regarded as a mystery, began to assume the shape of a crime. The wife openly accused the husband of never having liked the animal, and more than hinted that he and the gardener between them could give a tolerably truthful account of its last moments; an insinuation that the husband repudiated with a warmth that only added credence to the original surmise.

'The bull-terrier was had up and searchingly examined. Fortunately for him, he had not had a single fight for two whole days. Had any recent traces of blood been detected upon him, it would have gone hard with him.

'The person who suffered most, however, was the youngest boy. Three weeks before, he had dressed the cat in doll's clothes and taken it round the garden in the perambulator. He himself had forgotten the incident, but Justice, though tardy, was on his track. The misdeed was suddenly remembered at the very moment when unavailing regret for the loss of the favourite was at its deepest, so that to box his ears and send him, then and there, straight off to bed was felt to be a positive relief.

'At the end of a fortnight, the cat, finding he had not, after all, bettered himself, came back. The family were so surprised that at first they could not be sure whether he was flesh and blood, or a spirit come to comfort them. After watching him eat half a pound of raw steak, they decided he was material, and caught him up and hugged him to their bosoms. For a week they over-fed him and made much of him. Then, the excitement cooling, he found himself dropping back into his old position, and didn't like it, and went next door again.

'The next door people had also missed him, and they likewise greeted his return with extravagant ebullitions of joy. This gave the cat an idea. He saw that his game was to play the two families off one against the other; which he did. He spent an alternate fortnight with each, and lived like a fighting-cock. His return was always greeted with enthusiasm, and every means were adopted to induce him to stay. His little whims were carefully studied, his favourite dishes kept in constant readiness.

'The destination of his goings leaked out at length, and then the two families quarrelled about him over the fence. My friend accused the newspaper man of having lured him away. The newspaper man retorted that the poor creature had come to his door wet and starving, and added that he would be ashamed to keep an animal merely to illtreat it. They have a quarrel about him twice a week on the average. It will probably come to blows one of these days.'

Jephson appeared much surprised by this story. He remained thoughtful and silent. I asked him if he would like to hear any more, and as he offered no active opposition I went on. (Maybe he was asleep; that idea did not occur to me at the time.)

I told him of my grandmother's cat, who, after living a blameless life for upwards of eleven years, and bringing up a family of something like sixty-six, not counting those that died in infancy and the water-butt, took to drink in her old age, and was run over while in a state of intoxication (oh, the justice of it!) by a brewer's dray. I have read in temperance tracts that no dumb animal will touch a drop of alcoholic liquor. My advice is, if you wish to keep them respectable, don't give them a chance to get at it. I knew a pony —— But never mind him; we are talking about my grandmother's cat.

A leaky beer-tap was the cause of her downfall. A saucer used to be placed underneath it to catch the drippings. One day the cat, coming in thirsty, and finding nothing else to drink, lapped up a little, liked it, and lapped a little more, went away for half an hour, and came back and finished the saucerful. Then sat down beside it, and waited for it to fill again.

From that day till the hour she died, I don't believe that cat was ever once quite sober. Her days she passed in a drunken stupor before the kitchen fire. Her nights she spent in the beer cellar.

My grandmother, shocked and grieved beyond expression, gave up her barrel and adopted bottles. The cat, thus condemned to enforced abstinence, meandered about the house for a day and a half in a disconsolate, quarrelsome mood. Then she disappeared, returning at eleven o'clock as tight as a drum.

Where she went, and how she managed to procure the drink, we never discovered; but the same programme was repeated every day. Some time during the morning she would contrive to elude our vigilance and escape; and late every evening she would come reeling home across the fields in a condition that I will not sully my pen by attempting to describe.

It was on Saturday night that she met the sad end to which I have before alluded. She must have been very drunk, for the man told us that, in consequence of the darkness, and the fact that his horses were tired, he was proceeding at little more than a snail's pace.

I think my grandmother was rather relieved than otherwise. She had been very fond of the cat at one time, but its recent conduct had alienated her affection. We children buried it in the garden under the mulberry tree, but the old lady insisted that there should be no tombstone, not even a mound raised. So it lies there, unhonoured, in a drunkard's grave.

I also told him of another cat our family had once possessed. She was the most motherly thing I have ever known. She was never happy without a family. Indeed, I cannot remember her when she hadn't a family in one stage or another. She was not very particular what sort of a family it was. If she could not have kittens, then she would content herself with puppies or rats. Anything that she could wash and feed seemed to satisfy her. I believe she would have brought up chickens if we had entrusted them to her.

All her brains must have run to motherliness, for she hadn't much sense. She could never tell the difference between her own children and other people's. She thought everything young was a kitten. We once mixed up a spaniel puppy that had lost its own mother among her progeny. I shall never forget her astonishment when it first barked. She boxed both its ears, and then sat looking down at it with an expression of indignant sorrow that was really touching.

'You're going to be a credit to your mother,' she seemed to be saying; 'you're a nice comfort to any one's old age, you are, making a row like that. And look at your ears flopping all over your face. I don't know where you pick up such ways.'

He was a good little dog. He did try to mew, and he did try to wash his face with his paw, and to keep his tail still, but his success was not commensurate with his will. I do not know which was the sadder to reflect upon, his efforts to become a creditable kitten, or his foster-mother's despair of ever making him one.

Later on we gave her a baby squirrel to rear. She was nursing a family of her own at the time, but she adopted him with enthusiasm, under the impression that he was another kitten, though she could not quite make out how she had come to overlook him. He soon became her prime favourite. She liked his colour, and took a mother's pride in his tail. What troubled her was that it would cock up over his head. She would hold it down with one paw, and lick it by the half-hour together, trying to make it set properly. But the moment she let it go up it would cock again. I have heard her cry with vexation because of this.

One day a neighbouring cat came to see her, and the squirrel was clearly the subject of their talk.

'It's a good colour,' said the friend, looking critically at the supposed kitten, who was sitting up on his haunches combing his whiskers, and saying the only truthfully pleasant thing about him that she could think of.

'He's a lovely colour,' exclaimed our cat proudly.

'I don't like his legs much,' remarked the friend.

'No,' responded his mother thoughtfully, 'you're right there. His legs are his weak point. I can't say I think much of his legs myself.'

'Maybe they'll fill out later on,' suggested the friend, kindly.

'Oh, I hope so,' replied the mother, regaining her momentarily dashed cheerfulness. 'Oh yes, they'll come all right in time. And then look at his tail. Now, honestly, did you ever see a kitten with a finer tail?'

'Yes it's a good tail,' assented the other; 'but why do you do it up over his head?'

'I don't,' answered our cat. 'It goes that way. I can't make it out. I suppose it will come straight as he gets older.'

'It will be awkward if it don't,' said the friend.

'Oh, but I'm sure it will,' replied our cat. 'I must lick it more. It's a tail that wants a good deal of licking, you can see that.'

And for hours that afternoon, after the other cat had gone, she sat trimming it; and, at the end, when she lifted her paw off it, and it flew back again like a steel spring over the squirrel's head, she sat and gazed at it with feelings that only those among my readers who have been mothers themselves will be able to comprehend.

'What have I done,' she seemed to say – 'what have I done that this trouble should come upon me?'

Jephson roused himself on my completion of this anecdote and sat up.

'You and your friends appear to have been the possessors of some very remarkable cats,' he observed.

'Yes,' I answered, 'our family has been singularly fortunate in its cats.'

'Singularly so,' agreed Jephson; 'I have never met but one man from whom I have heard more wonderful cat talk than, at one time or another, I have heard from you.'

'Oh,' I said, not, perhaps without a touch of jealousy in my voice, 'and who was he?'

'He was a seafaring man,' replied Jephson. 'I met him on a Hampstead tram, and we discussed the subject of animal sagacity.

'"Yes, sir," he said, "monkeys is cute. I've come across monkeys as could give points to one or two lubbers I've sailed under; and elephants is pretty spry, if you can believe all that's told of 'em. I've heard some tall tales about elephants. And, of course, dogs has their heads screwed on all right: I don't say as they ain't. But what I do say is: that for straightfor'ard, level-headed reasoning, give me cats. You see, sir, a dog, he thinks a powerful deal of a man – never was such a cute thing as a man, in a dog's opinion; and he takes good care that everybody knows it. Naturally enough, we says a dog is the most intellectual animal there is. Now a cat, she's got her own opinion about human beings. She don't say much but you can tell enough to make you anxious not to hear the whole of it. The consequence is, we says a cat's got no intelligence. That's where we let our prejudice steer our judgment wrong. In a matter of plain common sense, there ain't a cat living as couldn't take the lee side of a dog and fly round him. Now, have you ever noticed a dog at the end of a chain, trying to kill a cat as is sitting washing her face three-quarters of an inch out of his reach? Of course you have. Well, who's got the sense out of those two? The cat knows that it ain't in the nature of steel chains to stretch. The dog, who ought, you'd think, to know a durned sight more about 'em than she does, is sure they will if you only bark loud enough.

'"Then again, have you ever been made mad by cats

screeching in the night, and jumped out of bed and opened the window and yelled at them? Did they ever budge an inch for that, though you shrieked loud enough to skeer the dead, and waved your arms about like a man in a play? Not they. They've turned and looked at you, that's all. 'Yell away, old man,' they've said, 'we like to hear you: the more the merrier.' Then what have you done? Why, you've snatched up a hairbrush, or a boot, or a candlestick, and made as if you'd throw it at them. They've seen your attitude, they've seen the thing in your hand, but they ain't moved a point. They knew as as you weren't going to chuck valuable property out of window with the chance of getting it lost or spoiled. They've got sense themselves, and they give you credit for having some. If you don't believe that's the reason, you try showing them a lump of coal, or half a brick next time – something as they know you *will* throw. Before you're ready to heave it, there won't be a cat within aim.

'"Then as to judgment and knowledge of the world, why dogs are babies to 'em. Have you ever tried telling a yarn before a cat, sir?"

'I replied that cats had often been present during anecdotal recitals of mine, but that, hitherto, I had paid no particular attention to their demeanour.

'"Ah, well, you take an opportunity of doing so one day, sir," answered the old fellow; "it's worth the experiment. If you're telling a story before a cat, and she don't get uneasy during any part of the narrative, you can reckon you've got hold of a thing as it will be safe for you to tell to the Lord Chief Justice of England.

"'I've got a messmate," he continued; "William Cooley is his name. We call him Truthful Billy. He's as good a seaman as ever trod quarter-deck; but when he gets spinning yarns he ain't the sort of man as I could advise you to rely upon. Well, Billy, he's got a dog, and I've seen him sit and tell yarns before that dog that would make a cat squirm out of its skin, and that dog's taken 'em in and believed 'em. One night, up at his old woman's, Bill told us a yarn by the side of which salt junk two voyages old would pass for spring chicken. I watched the dog to see how he would take it. He listened to it from beginning to end with cocked ears, and  never so much as blinked. Every now and then he would look round with an expression of astonishment or delight that seemed to say: 'Wonderful, isn't it!' 'Dear me, just think of it!' 'Did you ever!' 'Well, if that don't beat everything!' He was a chuckle-headed dog; you could have told him anything.

"'It irritated me that Bill should have such an animal about him to encourage him, and when he had finished I said to him, 'I wish you'd tell that yarn round at my quarters one evening.'

"'Why?' said Bill.

"'Oh, it's just a fancy of mine," I says. I didn't tell him I was wanting my old cat to hear it.

"'Oh, all right,' says Bill, "you remind me." He loved yarning, Billy did.

"'Next night but one he slings himself up in my cabin, and I does so. Nothing loth, off he starts. There was about half-a-dozen of us stretched round, and the cat was sitting before the fire fussing itself up. Before Bill had got fairly under weigh, she stops washing and looks up at me, puzzled like, as much as to say, 'What have we got here, a missionary?' I signalled to her to keep quiet, and Bill went on with his yarn. When he got to the part about the sharks, she turned deliberately round and looked at him. I tell you there was an expression of disgust on that cat's face as might have made a travelling Cheap Jack feel ashamed of himself. It was that human, I give you my word, sir, I forgot for the moment as the poor animal couldn't speak. I could see the words that were on its lips: 'Why don't you tell us you swallowed the anchor?' and I sat on tenter-hooks, fearing each instant that she would say them aloud. It was a relief to me when she turned her back on Bill.

'"For a few minutes she sat very still, and seemed to be wrestling with herself like. I never saw a cat more set on controlling its feelings, or that seemed to suffer more in silence. It made my heart ache to watch it.

'"At last Bill came to the point where he and the captain between 'em hold the shark's mouth open while the cabin-boy dives in head foremost, and fetches up, undigested, the gold watch and chain as the bo'sun was a-wearing when he fell overboard; and at that the old cat giv'd a screech, and rolled over on her side with her legs in the air.

"'I thought at first the poor thing was dead, but she rallied after a bit, and it seemed as though she had braced herself up to hear the thing out.

"'But a little further on, Bill got too much for her again, and this time she owned herself beat. She rose up and looked round at us: 'You'll excuse me, gentlemen,' she said – leastways that is what she said if looks go for anything – 'maybe you're used to this sort of rubbish, and it don't get on your nerves. With me it's different. I guess I've heard as much of this fool's talk as my constitution will stand, and if it's all the same to you I'll get outside before I'm sick.'

"'With that she walked up to the door, and I opened it for her, and she went out.

"'You can't fool a cat with talk same as you can a dog.'"

CHAPTER VII

Does man ever reform? Balzac says he doesn't. So far as my experience goes, it agrees with that of Balzac – a fact the admirers of that author are at liberty to make what use of they please.

When I was young and accustomed to take my views of life from people who were older than myself, and who knew better, so they said, I used to believe that he did. Examples of 'reformed characters' were frequently pointed out to me – indeed, our village, situate a few miles from a small seaport town, seemed to be peculiarly rich in such. They were, from all accounts, including their own, persons who had formerly behaved with quite unnecessary depravity, and who, at the time I knew them, appeared to be going to equally objectionable lengths in the opposite direction. They invariably belonged to one of two classes, the low-spirited or the aggressively unpleasant. They said, and I believed, that they were happy; but I could not help reflecting how very sad they must have been before they were happy.

One of them, a small, meek-eyed old man with a piping voice, had been exceptionally wild in his youth. What had been his special villainy I could never discover. People responded to my inquiries by saying that he had been 'Oh, generally bad,' and increased my longing for detail by adding that little boys ought not to want to know about such things. From their tone and manner I assumed that he must have been a pirate at the very least, and regarded him with awe, not unmingled with secret admiration.

Whatever it was, he had been saved from it by his wife, a

bony lady of unprepossessing appearance, but irreproachable views.

One day he called at our house for some purpose or other, and, being left alone with him for a few minutes, I took the opportunity of interviewing him personally on the subject.

'You were very wicked once, weren't you?' I said, seeking by emphasis on the 'once' to mitigate what I felt might be the disagreeable nature of the question.

To my intense surprise, a gleam of shameful glory lit up his wizened face, and a sound which I tried to think a sigh, but which sounded like a chuckle, escaped his lips.

'Ay,' he replied; 'I've been a bit of a spanker in my time.'

The term 'spanker' in such connection puzzled me. I had hitherto led to regard a spanker as an eminently conscientious person, especially where the short-comings of other people were concerned; a person who laboured for the good of others. That the word could also be employed to designate a sinful party was a revelation to me.

'But you are good now, aren't you?' I continued, dismissing further reflection upon the etymology of 'spanker' to a more fitting occasion.

'Ay, ay,' he answered, his countenance resuming its customary aspect of resigned melancholy. 'I be a brand plucked from the burning, I be. There beant much wrong wi' Deacon Sawyers, now.'

'And it was your wife that made you good, wasn't it?' I persisted, determined, now that I had started this investigation, to obtain confirmation at first hand on all points.

At the mention of his wife his features became suddenly transformed. Glancing hurriedly round, to make sure, apparently, that no one but myself was within hearing, he leaned across and hissed these words into my ear – I have never forgotten them, there was a ring of such evident sincerity about them——

'I'd like to skin her, I'd like to skin her alive.'

It struck me, even in the light of my then limited judgment, as an unregenerate wish; and thus early my faith in the possibility of man's reformation received the first of those many blows that have resulted in shattering it.

Nature, whether human or otherwise, was not made to be reformed. You can develop, you can check, but you cannot alter it.

You can take a small tiger and train it to sit on a hearthrug, and to lap milk, and so long as you provide it with hearthrugs to lie on and sufficient milk to drink, it will purr and behave like an affectionate domestic pet. But it is a tiger, with all a tiger's instincts, and its progeny to the end of all time will be tigers.

In the same way, you can take an ape and develop it through a few thousand generations until it loses its tail and becomes an altogether superior ape. You can go on developing it through still a few more thousands of generations until it gathers to itself out of the waste vapours of eternity an intellect and a soul, by the aid of which it is enabled to keep the original apish nature more or less under control.

But the ape is still there, and always will be, and every now and again, when Constable Civilisation turns his back for a moment, as during 'Spanish Furies,' or 'September massacres,' or Western mob rule, it creeps out and bites and tears at quivering flesh, or plunges its hairy arms elbow deep in blood, or dances round a burning nigger.

I knew a man once – or, rather, I knew of a man – who was a confirmed drunkard. He became and continued a drunkard, not through weakness, but through will. When his friends remonstrated with him, he told them to mind their own business, and to let him mind his. If he saw any reason for not getting drunk he would give it up. Meanwhile he liked getting drunk, and he meant to get drunk as often as possible.

He went about it deliberately, and did it thoroughly. For nearly ten years, so it was reported, he never went to bed sober. This may be an exaggeration – it would be a singular report were it not – but it can be relied upon as sufficiently truthful for all practical purposes.

Then there came a day when he did see a reason for not getting drunk. He signed no pledge, he took no oath. He said, 'I will never touch another drop of drink' and for twenty-six years he kept his word.

At the end of that time a combination of circumstances occurred that made life troublesome to him, so that he desired to be rid of it altogether. He was a man accustomed, when he desired a thing within his reach, to stretch out his hand and take it. He reviewed the case calmly, and decided to commit suicide.

If the thing were to be done at all, it would be best, for reasons that if set forth would make this a long story, that it should be done that very night, and, if possible, before eleven o'clock, which was the earliest hour a certain person could arrive from a certain place.

It was then four in the afternoon. He attended to some necessary business, and wrote some necessary letters. This occupied him until seven. He then called a cab and drove to a small hotel in the suburbs, engaged a private room, and ordered up materials for the making of the particular punch that had been the last beverage he had got drunk on, six-and-twenty years ago.

For three hours he sat there drinking steadily, with his watch before him. At half-past ten he rang the bell, paid his bill, came home, and cut his throat.

For a quarter of a century people had been calling that man a 'reformed character.' His character had not reformed one jot. The craving for drink had never died. For twenty-six years he had, being a great man, held it gripped by the throat. When all things became a matter of indifference to him, he loosened his grasp, and the evil instinct rose up within him as strong on the day he died as on the day he forced it down.

That is all a man can do, pray for strength to crush down the evil that is in him, and to keep it held down day after day. I never hear washy talk about 'changed characters' and 'reformed natures' but I think of a sermon I once heard at a Wesleyan revivalist meeting in the Black Country.

'Ah! my friends, we've all of us got the devil inside us. I've got him, you've got him,' cried the preacher – he was an old man, with long white hair and beard, and wild, fighting eyes. Most of the preachers who came 'reviving,' as it was called, through that district, had those eyes. Some of them needed 'reviving' themselves, in quite another sense, before they got clear out of it. I am speaking now of more than thirty years ago.

'Ah! so us have – so us have,' came the response.

'And you carn't get rid of him,' continued the speaker.

'Not of oursel's,' ejaculated a fervent voice at the end of the room, 'but the Lord will help us.'

The old preacher turned on him almost fiercely:–

'But th' Lord woan't,' he shouted; 'doan't 'ee reckon on that, lad. Ye've got him an' ye've got ta keep him. Ye carn't get rid of him. Th' Lord doan't mean 'ee to.'

Here there broke forth murmurs of angry disapproval, but the old fellow went on, unheeding:–

'It arn't good for 'ee to get rid of him. Ye've just got to hug him tight. Doan't let him go. Hold him fast, and – LAM INTO HIM. I tell 'ee it's good, healthy Christian exercise.'

We had been discussing the subject with reference to our hero. It had been suggested by Brown as an unhackneyed idea, and one lending itself, therefore, to comparative freshness of treatment, that our hero should be a thorough-paced scamp.

Jephson seconded the proposal, for the reason that it would the better enable us to accomplish artistic work. He was of opinion that we should be more sure of our ground in drawing a villain than in attempting to portray a good man.

MacShaughnassy thirded (if I may coin what has often

appeared to me to be a much-needed word) the motion with ardour. He was tired, he said, of the crystal-hearted, noble-thinking young man of fiction. Besides, it made bad reading for the 'young person.' It gave her false ideas, and made her dissatisfied with mankind as he really is.

And, thereupon, he launched forth and sketched us his idea of a hero, with reference to whom I can only say that I should not like to meet him on a dark night.

An out-and-out blackguard completely reformed

Brown, our one earnest member, begged us to be reasonable, and reminded us, not for the first time, and not, perhaps, altogether unnecessarily, that these meetings were for the purpose of discussing business, not of talking nonsense.

Thus adjured, we attacked the subject conscientiously.

Brown's idea was that the man should be an out-and-out blackguard, until about the middle of the book, when some event should transpire that would have the effect of completely reforming him. This naturally brought the discussion down to the question with which I have commenced this chapter: Does man ever reform? I argued in the negative, and gave the reasons for my disbelief much as I have set them forth here. MacShaughnassy, on the other hand, contended that he did, and instanced the case of himself – a man who, in his early days, so he asserted, had been a scatterbrained, impracticable person, entirely without stability.

I maintained that this was merely an example of enormous will-power enabling a man to overcome and rise superior to the defects of character with which nature had handicapped him.

'My opinion of you,' I said, 'is that you are naturally a hopelessly irresponsible, well-meaning ass. But,' I continued quickly, seeing his hand reaching out towards a complete Shakespeare in one volume that lay upon the piano, 'your mental capabilities are of such extraordinary power that you can disguise this fact, and make yourself appear a man of sense and wisdom.'

Brown agreed with me that in MacShaughnassy's case traces of the former disposition were clearly apparent, but pleaded that the illustration was an unfortunate one, and that it ought not to have weight in the discussion.

'Seriously speaking,' said he, 'don't you think that there are some experiences great enough to break up and re-form a man's nature?'

'To break up,' I replied, 'yes; but to re-form, no. Passing through a great experience may shatter a man, or it may strengthen a man, just as passing through a furnace may melt or purify metal, but no furnace ever lit upon this earth can change a bar of gold into a bar of lead, or a bar of lead into one of gold.'

I asked Jephson what he thought. He did not consider the bar of gold simile a good one. He held that a man's character was not an immutable element. He likened it to a drug – poison or elixir – compounded by each man for himself from the pharmacopoeia of all things known to life and time, and saw no impossibility, though some improbability, in the glass being flung aside and a fresh draught prepared with pain and labour.

'Well,' I said, 'let us put the case practically; did you ever know a man's character to change?'

'Yes,' he answered, 'I did know a man whose character seemed to me to be completely changed by an experience that happened to him. It may, as you say, only have been that he was shattered, or that the lesson may have taught him to keep his natural disposition ever under control. The result, in any case, was striking.'

We asked him to give us the history of the case, and he did so.

'He was a friend of some cousins of mine,' Jephson began, 'people I used to see a good deal of in my undergraduate days. When I met him first he was a young fellow of twenty-six, strong mentally and physically, and of a stern and stubborn nature that those who liked him called masterful, and that those who disliked him – a more numerous body – termed tyrannical. When I saw him three years later, he was an old man of twenty-nine, gentle and yielding beyond the border-line of weakness, mistrustful of himself and considerate of others to a degree that was often unwise. Formerly, his anger had been a thing very easily and frequently aroused. Since the change of which I speak, I have never known the shade of anger to cross his face but once. In the course of a walk, one day, we came upon a young rough terrifying a small child by pretending to set a dog at her. He seized the boy with a grip that almost choked him, and administered to him a punishment that seemed to me altogether out of proportion to the crime, brutal though it was.

'I remonstrated with him when he rejoined me.

'"Yes," he replied apologetically; "I suppose I'm a hard judge of some follies." And, knowing what his haunted eyes were looking at, I said no more.

'He was junior partner in a large firm of tea brokers in the City. There was not much for him to do in the London office, and when, therefore, as the result of some mortgage transactions, a South Indian tea plantation fell into the hands of the firm, it was suggested that he should go out and take the management of it. The plan suited him admirably. He was a man in every way qualified to lead a rough life; to face a by no means contemptible amount of difficulty and danger, to govern a small army of native workers more amenable to fear than to affection. Such a life, demanding thought and action, would afford his strong nature greater interest and enjoyment than he could ever hope to obtain amid the cramped surroundings of civilisation.

'Only one thing could in reason have been urged against the

arrangement, that thing was his wife. She was a fragile, delicate girl, whom he had married in obedience to that instinct of attraction towards the opposite which Nature, for the purpose of maintaining her average, has implanted in our breasts – a timid, meek-eyed creature, one of those women to whom death is less terrible than danger, and fate easier to face than fear. Such women have been known to run screaming from a house and to meet martyrdom with heroism. They can no more keep their nerves from trembling than an aspen tree can stay the quivering of its leaves.

'That she was totally unfitted for, and would be made wretched by the life to which

'She was a fragile, delicate girl'

his acceptance of the post would condemn her might have readily occurred to him, had he stopped to consider for a moment her feelings in the matter. But to view a question from any other standpoint than his own was not his habit. That he loved her passionately, in his way, as a thing belonging to himself, there can be no doubt, but it was with the love that such men have for the dog they will thrash, the horse they will spur to a broken back. To consult her on the subject never entered his head. He informed her one day of his decision and of the date of the sailing, and, handing her a handsome cheque, told her to purchase all things necessary to her, and to let him know if she needed more; and she, loving him with a dog-like devotion that was not good for him, opened her big eyes a little wider, but said nothing. She thought much about the coming change to herself, however, and, when nobody was by, she would cry softly; then, hearing his footsteps, would hastily wipe away the traces of her tears, and go to meet him with a smile.

'Now, her timidity and nervousness, which at home had been a butt for mere chaff, became, under the new circumstances of their life, a serious annoyance to the man. A woman who seemed unable to repress a scream whenever she turned and saw in the gloom a pair of piercing eyes looking out at her from a dusky face, who was liable to drop off her horse with fear at the sound of a wild beast's roar a mile off, and who would turn white and limp with horror at the mere sight of a snake, was not a companionable person to live with in the neighbourhood of Indian jungles.

'He himself was entirely without fear, and could not understand it. To him it was pure affectation. He had a muddled idea, common to men of his stamp, that women assume nervousness because they think it pretty and becoming to them, and that if one could only convince them of the folly of it they might be induced to lay it aside, in the same way that they lay aside mincing steps and simpering voices. A man who prided himself, as he did, upon his knowledge of horses, might, one would think, have grasped a truer notion of the nature of nervousness, which is a mere matter of temperament. But the man was a fool.

'The thing that vexed him most was her horror of snakes. He was unblessed – or uncursed, whichever you may prefer – with imagination of any kind. There was no special enmity between him and the seed of the serpent. A creature that crawled upon its belly was no more terrible to him than a creature that walked upon its legs; indeed, less so, for he knew that, as a rule, there was less danger to be apprehended from them. A reptile is only too eager at all times to escape from man. Unless attacked or frightened, it will make no onset. Most people are content to acquire their knowledge of this fact from the natural history books. He had proved it for himself. His servant, an old sergeant of dragoons, has told me that he has seen him stop with his face six inches from the head of a hooded cobra, and stand watching it through his eye-glass as it crawled away from him, knowing that one touch of its fangs would mean death from which there could be no possible escape. That any reasoning being should be inspired with terror – sickening, deadly terror – by such pitifully harmless things, seemed to him monstrous; and he determined to try and cure her of her fear of them.

'He succeeded in doing this eventually somewhat more thoroughly than he had anticipated, but it left a terror in his own eyes that has not gone out of them to this day, and that never will.

'One evening, riding home through a part of the jungle not far from his bungalow, he heard a soft, low hiss close to his ear, and, looking up, saw a python swing itself from the branch of a tree and make off through the long grass. He had been out antelope-shooting, and his loaded rifle hung by his stirrup. Springing from the frightened horse, he was just in time to get a shot at the creature before it disappeared. He had hardly expected, under the circumstances, to even hit it. By chance the bullet struck it at the junction of the vertebrae with the head, and killed it instantly. It was a well-marked specimen, and, except for the small wound the bullet had made, quite uninjured. He picked it up, and hung it across the saddle, intending to take it home and preserve it.

'Galloping along, glancing down every now and again at the huge, hideous thing swaying and writhing in front of him almost as if still alive, a brilliant idea occurred to him. He would use this dead reptile to cure his wife of her fear of living ones. He would fix matters so that she should see it, and think it was alive, and be terrified by it; then he would show her that she had been frightened by a mere dead thing, and she would feel ashamed of herself, and be healed of her folly. It was the sort of idea that would occur to a fool.

'When he reached home, he took the dead snake into his smoking-room; then, locking the door, the idiot set out his prescription. He arranged the monster in a very natural and life-like position. It appeared to be crawling from the open window across the floor, and any one coming into the room suddenly could hardly avoid treading on it. It was very cleverly done.

'That finished, he picked out a book from the shelves, opened it, and laid it face downward upon the couch. When he had completed all things to his satisfaction he unlocked the door and came out, very pleased with himself.

'After dinner he lit a cigar and sat smoking a while in silence.

'"Are you feeling tired?" he said to her at length, with a smile.

'She laughed, and, calling him a lazy old thing, asked what it was he wanted.

'"Only my novel that I was reading. I left it in my den. Do you mind? You will find it open on the couch."

'She sprang up and ran lightly to the door.

'As she paused there for a moment to look back at him and

ask the name of the book, he thought how pretty and how sweet she was; and for the first time a faint glimmer of the true nature of the thing he was doing forced itself into his brain.

'"Never mind," he said, half rising, "I'll——"; then, enamoured of the brilliancy of his plan, checked himself; and she was gone.

'He heard her footsteps passing along the matted passage, and smiled to himself. He thought the affair was going to be rather amusing. One finds it difficult to pity him even now when one thinks of it.

'The smoking-room door opened and closed, and he still sat gazing dreamily at the ash of his cigar, and smiling.

'One moment, perhaps two passed, but the time seemed much longer. The man blew the gray cloud from before his eyes and waited. Then he heard what he had been expecting to hear – a piercing shriek. Then another, which, expecting to hear the clanging of the distant door and the scurrying back of her footsteps along the passage, puzzled him, so that the smile died away from his lips.

'Then another, and another, and another, shriek after shriek.

'The native servant, gliding noiselessly about the room, laid down the thing that was in his hand and moved instinctively towards the door. The man started up and held him back.

'"Keep where you are," he said hoarsely. "It is nothing. Your mistress is frightened, that is all. She must learn to get over this folly." Then he listened again, and the shrieks ended with what sounded curiously like a smothered laugh; and there came a sudden silence.

'And out of that bottomless silence, Fear for the first time in his life came to the man, and he and the dusky servant looked at each other with eyes in which there was a strange likeness; and by a common instinct moved together towards the place where the silence came from.

'When the man opened the door he saw three things: one

was the dead python, lying where he had left it; the second was a live python, its comrade apparently, slowly crawling round it; the third a crushed, bloody heap in the middle of the floor.

'He himself remembered nothing more until, weeks afterwards, he opened his eyes in a darkened, unfamiliar place, but the native servant, before he fled screaming from the house, saw his master fling himself upon the living serpent and grasp it with his hands, and when, later on, others burst into the room and caught him staggering in their arms, they found the second python with its head torn off.

'That is the incident that changed the character of my man – if it be changed,' concluded Jephson. 'He told it me one night as we sat on the deck of the steamer, returning from Bombay. He did not spare himself. He told me the story, much as I have told it to you, but in an even, monotonous tone, free from emotion of any kind. I asked him, when he had finished, how he could bear to recall it.

'"Recall it!" he replied, with a slight accent of surprise; "it is always with me."'

CHAPTER VIII

One day we spoke of crime and criminals. We had discussed the possibility of a novel without a villain, but had decided that it would be uninteresting.

'It is a terribly sad reflection,' remarked MacShaughnassy, musingly; 'but what a desperately dull place this earth would be if it were not for our friends the bad people. Do you know,' he continued, 'when I hear of folks going about trying to reform everybody and make them good, I get positively nervous. Once do away with sin, and literature will become a thing of the past. Without the criminal classes we authors would starve.'

'I shouldn't worry,' replied Jephson, drily; 'one half mankind has been "reforming" the other half pretty steadily ever since the Creation, yet there appears to be a fairly appreciable amount of human nature left in it, notwithstanding. Suppressing sin is much the same sort of task that suppressing a volcano would be – plugging one vent merely opens another. Evil will last our time.'

'I cannot take your optimistic view of the case,' answered MacShaughnassy. 'It seems to me that crime – at all events, interesting crime – is being slowly driven out of our existence. Pirates and highwaymen have been practically abolished. Dear old "Smuggler Bill" has melted down his cutlass into a pint-can with a false bottom. The pressgang that was always so ready to rescue our hero from his approaching marriage has been disbanded. There's not a lugger fit for the purposes of abduction left upon the coast. Men settle their "affairs of honour" in the law courts, and return home wounded only in the pocket. Assaults on unprotected females are confined to the slums, where heroes do not dwell, and are avenged by the nearest magistrate. Your modern burglar is generally an out-of-work green-grocer. His "swag" usually consists of an overcoat and a pair of boots, in attempting to make off with which he is captured by the servant-girl. Suicides and murders are getting scarcer every season. At the present rate of decrease, deaths by violence will be unheard of in another decade, and a murder story will be laughed at as too improbable to be interesting. A certain section of busybodies are even crying out for the enforcement of the seventh commandment. If they succeed authors will have to follow the advice generally given to them by the critics, and retire from business altogether. I tell you our means of livelihood are being filched from us one by one. Authors ought to form themselves into a society for the support and encouragement of crime.'

MacShaughnassy's leading intention in making these remarks was to shock and grieve Brown, and in this object he succeeded. Brown is – or was, in those days – an earnest young man with an exalted – some were inclined to say an exaggerated – view of the importance and dignity of the literary profession. Brown's notion of the scheme of Creation was that God made the universe so as to give the literary man something to write about. I used at one time to credit Brown with originality for this idea; but as I have grown older I have learned that the theory is a very common and popular one in cultured circles.

Brown expostulated with MacShaughnassy. 'You speak,' he said, 'as though literature were the parasite of evil.'

'And what else is she?' replied the MacShaughnassy, with enthusiasm. 'What would become of literature without folly and sin? What is the work of the literary man but raking a living for himself out of the dust-heap of human woe? Imagine, if you can, a perfect world – a world where men and women never said foolish things and never did unwise ones; where small boys were never mischievous and children never made awkward remarks; where dogs never fought and cats never screeched; where wives never henpecked their husbands and mothers-in-law never nagged; where men never went to bed in their boots and sea-captains never swore; where plumbers understood their work and old maids never dressed as girls; where niggers never stole chickens and proud men were never sea-sick! where would be your humour and your wit? Imagine a world where hearts were never bruised; where lips were never pressed with pain; where eyes were never dim; where feet were never weary; where stomachs were never empty! where would be your pathos? Imagine a world where husbands never loved more wives than one, and that the right one; where wives were never kissed but by their husbands; where men's hearts were never black and women's thoughts never impure; where there was no hating and no envying; no desiring; no despairing! where would be your scenes of passion, your interesting complications, your subtle psychological analyses? My dear Brown, we writers – novelists, dramatists, poets – we fatten on the misery of our fellow-creatures. God created man and woman, and the woman created the literary man when she put her teeth into the apple. We came into the world under the shadow of the serpent. We are special correspondents with the Devil's army. We report his victories in our three-volume novels, his occasional defeats in our five-act melodramas.'

'All of which is very true,' remarked Jephson; 'but you must remember it is not only the literary man who traffics in misfortune. The doctor, the lawyer, the preacher, the newspaper proprietor, the weather prophet, will hardly, I should say, welcome the millennium. I shall never forget an anecdote my uncle used to relate, dealing with the period when he was chaplain of the Lincolnshire county jail. One morning there was to be a hanging; and the usual little crowd of witnesses, consisting of the sheriff, the governor, three or four reporters, a magistrate, and a couple of warders, was assembled in the prison. The condemned man, a brutal ruffian who had been found guilty of murdering a young girl under exceptionally revolting circumstances, was being pinioned by the hangman and his assistant; and my uncle was employing the last few moments at his disposal in trying to break down the sullen indifference the fellow had throughout manifested towards both his crime and his fate.

'My uncle failing to make any impression upon him, the governor ventured to add a few words of exhortation, upon which the man turned fiercely on the whole of them.

'"Go to hell," he cried, "with your snivelling jaw. Who are you, to preach at me? *You're* glad enough I'm here – all of you. Why, I'm the only one of you as ain't going to make a bit over this job. Where would you all be, I should like to know, you canting swine, if it wasn't for me and my sort? Why, it's the likes of me as *keeps* the likes of you," with which he walked straight to the gallows and told the hangman to "hurry up" and not keep the gentlemen waiting.'

'There was some "grit" in that man,' said MacShaughnassy.

'Yes,' added Jephson, 'and wholesome wit also.'

MacShaughnassy puffed a mouthful of smoke over a spider which was just about to kill a fly. This caused the spider to fall into the river, from where a supper-hunting swallow quickly rescued him.

'You remind me,' he said 'of a scene I once witnessed in the office of *The Daily* —— well, in the office of a certain daily newspaper. It was the dead season, and things were somewhat slow. An endeavour had been made to launch a discussion on the question "Are Babies a Blessing?" The youngest reporter on the staff, writing over the simple but touching signature of "Mother of Six," had led off with a scathing, though somewhat irrelevant, attack upon husbands, as a class; the Sporting Editor, signing himself "Working Man," and garnishing his contribution with painfully elaborated orthographical lapses, arranged to give an air of verisimilitude to the correspondence, while, at the same time, not to offend the susceptibilities of the democracy (from whom the paper derived its chief support), had replied, vindicating the British father, and giving what purported to be stirring midnight experiences of his own. The Gallery Man, calling himself, with a burst of imagination, "Gentleman and Christian," wrote indignantly that he considered the agitation of the subject to be both impious and indelicate, and added he was surprised that a paper holding the exalted, and deservedly popular, position of *The* —— should have opened its columns to the brainless vapourings of "Mother of Six" and "Working Man."

'The topic had, however, fallen flat. With the exception of one man who had invented a new feeding-bottle, and thought he was going to advertise it for nothing, the outside public did not respond, and over the editorial department gloom had settled down.

'One evening, as two or three of us were mooning about the stairs, praying secretly for a war or a famine, Todhunter, the town reporter, rushed past us with a cheer, and burst into the Sub-editor's room. We followed. He was waving his notebook above his head, and clamouring, after the manner of people in French exercises, for pens, ink, and paper.

'"What's up?" cried the Sub-editor, catching his enthusiasm; "influenza again?"

'"Better than that!" shouted Todhunter. "Excursion steamer run down, a hundred and twenty-five lives lost – four good columns of heartrending scenes."

'"By Jove!" said the Sub, "couldn't have happened at a better time either" – and then he sat down and dashed off a leaderette, in which he dwelt upon the pain and regret the paper felt at having to announce the disaster, and drew attention to the exceptionally harrowing account provided by the energy and talent of "our special reporter."'

'It is the law of nature,' said Jephson: 'we are not the first party of young philosophers who have been struck with the fact that one man's misfortune is another man's opportunity.'

'Occasionally, another woman's,' I observed.

I was thinking of an incident told me by a nurse. If a nurse in fair practice does not know more about human nature – does not see clearer into the souls of men and women than all the novelists in little Bookland put together – it must be because she is physically blind and deaf. All the world's a stage, and all the men and women merely players; so long as we are in good health, we play our parts out bravely to the end, acting them, on the whole, artistically and with strenuousness, even to the extent of sometimes fancying ourselves the people we are pretending to be. But with sickness comes forgetfulness of our part, and carelessness of the impression we are making upon the audience. We are too weak to put the paint and powder on our faces, the stage finery lies unheeded by our side. The heroic gestures, the virtuous sentiments are a weariness to us. In the quiet, darkened room, where the footlights of the great stage no longer glare upon us, where our ears are no longer strained to catch the clapping or the hissing of the town, we are, for a brief space, ourselves.

This nurse was a quiet, demure little woman, with a pair of dreamy, soft gray eyes that had a curious power of absorbing everything that passed before them without seeming to look at anything. Gazing upon much life, laid bare, had given to them a slightly cynical expression, but there was a background of kindliness behind.

During the evenings of my convalescence she would talk to me of her nursing experiences. I have sometimes thought I would put down in writing the stories that she told me, but they would be sad reading. The majority of them, I fear, would show only the tangled, seamy side of human nature, and God knows there is little need for us to point that out to each other, though so many nowadays seem to think it the only work worth doing. A few of them were sweet, but I think they were the saddest; and over one or two a man might laugh, but it would not be a pleasant laugh.

'I never enter the door of a house to which I have been summoned,' she said to me one evening, 'without wondering, as I step over the threshold, what the story is going to be. I always feel inside a sick-room as if I were behind the scenes of life. The people come and go about you, and you listen to them talking and laughing, and you look into your patient's eyes, and you just know that it's all a play.'

The incident that Jephson's remark had reminded me of, she told me one afternoon, as I sat propped up by the fire, trying to drink a glass of port wine, and feeling somewhat depressed at discovering I did not like it.

'One of my first cases,' she said, 'was a surgical operation. I was very young at the time, and I made rather an awkward mistake – I don't mean a professional mistake – but a mistake nevertheless that I ought to have had more sense than to make.

'My patient was a good-looking, pleasant-spoken gentleman. The wife was a pretty, dark little woman, but I never liked her from the first; she was one of those perfectly proper, frigid women, who always give me the idea that they were born in a church, and have never got over the chill. However, she seemed very fond of him, and he of her; and they talked very prettily to each other – too prettily for it to be quite genuine, I should have said, if I'd known as much of the world then as I do now.

'The operation was a difficult and dangerous one. When I came on duty in the evening I found him, as I expected, highly delirious. I kept him as quiet as I could, but towards nine o'clock, as the delirium only increased, I began to get anxious. I bent down close to him and listened to his ravings. Over and over again I heard the name "Louise". Why wouldn't "Louise" come to him? It was so unkind of her – they had dug a great pit, and were pushing him down into it – oh! why didn't she come and save him? He should be saved if she would only come and take his hand.

'His cries became so pitiful that I could bear them no longer.

His wife had gone to attend a prayer-meeting, but the church was only in the next street. Fortunately, the day-nurse had not left the house: I called her in to watch him for a minute, and, slipping on my bonnet, ran across. I told my errand to one of the vergers, and he took me to her. She was kneeling, but I could not wait.

'She was kneeling'

I pushed open the pew door, and, bending down, whispered to her, "Please come over at once; your husband is more delirious than I quite care about, and you may be able to calm him."

'She whispered back, without raising her head, "I'll be over in a little while. The meeting won't last much longer."

'Her answer surprised and nettled me. "You'll be acting more like a Christian woman by coming home with me," I said sharply, "than by stopping here. He keeps calling for you, and I can't get him to sleep."

'She raised her head from her hands: "Calling for me?" she asked with a slightly incredulous accent.

'"Yes," I replied, "it has been his one cry for the last hour: Where's Louise, why doesn't Louise come to him."

'Her face was in shadow, but as she turned it away, and the faint light from one of the turned-down gas-jets fell across it, I fancied I saw a smile upon it, and I disliked her more than ever.

'"I'll come back with you," she said, rising and putting her books away, and we left the church together.

'She asked me many questions on the way: Did patients, when they were delirious, know the people about them? Did they remember actual facts, or was their talk mere incoherent rambling? Could one guide their thoughts in any way?

'The moment we were inside the door, she flung off her bonnet and cloak, and came upstairs quickly and softly.

'She walked to the bedside, and stood looking down at him, but he was quite unconscious of her presence, and continued muttering. I suggested that she should speak to him, but she said she was sure it would be useless, and drawing a chair back into the shadow, sat down beside him.

'Seeing she was no good to him, I tried to persuade her to go to bed, but she said she would rather stop, and I, being little more than a girl then, and without much authority, let her. All night long he tossed and raved, the one name on his lips being ever Louise – Louise – and all night long that woman sat there in the shadow, never moving, never speaking, with a set smile on her lips that made me long to take her by the shoulders and shake her.

'At one time he imagined himself back in his courting days, and pleaded, "Say you love me, Louise. I know you do. I can read it in your eyes. What's the use of our pretending? We *know* each other. Put your white arms about me. Let me feel your breath upon my neck. Ah! I knew it, my darling, my love!"

'The whole of the house was deadly still, and I could hear every word of his troubled ravings. I almost felt as if I had no right to be there, listening to them, but my duty held me. Later on, he fancied himself planning a holiday with her, so I concluded. "I shall start on Monday evening," he was saying, "and you can join me in Dublin at Jackson's Hotel on the Wednesday, and we'll go straight on."

'His voice grew a little faint, and his wife moved forward on her chair, and bent her head closer to his lips.

'"No, no," he continued, after a pause, "there's no danger whatever. It's a lonely little place, right in the heart of the Galway Mountains – O'Mullen's Halfway House they call it – five miles from Ballynahinch. We shan't meet a soul there. We'll have three weeks of heaven all to ourselves, my goddess, my Mrs Maddox from Boston – don't forget the name."

'He laughed in his delirium; and the woman, sitting by his side, laughed also; and then the truth flashed across me.

'I ran up to her and caught her by the arm. "Your name's not Louise," I said, looking straight at her. It was an impertinent interference, but I felt excited, and acted on impulse.

'"No," she replied, very quietly; "but it's the name of a very dear school friend of mine. I've got the clue to-night that I've been waiting two years to get. Good-night, nurse, thanks for fetching me."

'She rose and went out, and I listened to her footsteps going down the stairs, and then drew up the blind and let in the dawn.

'I've never told that incident to any one until this evening,' my nurse concluded, as she took the empty port wine glass out of my hand, and stirred the fire. 'A nurse wouldn't get many engagements if she had the reputation for making blunders of that sort.'

'I listened to her footsteps going down the stairs'

Another story that she told me showed married life more lovelit, but then, as she added, with that cynical twinkle which glinted so oddly from her gentle, demure eyes, this couple had only very recently been wed – had, in fact, only just returned from their honeymoon.

They had been travelling on the Continent, and there had both contracted typhoid fever, which showed itself immediately on their home-coming.

'I was called in to them on the very day of their arrival,' she said; 'the husband was the first to take to his bed, and the wife followed suit twelve hours afterwards. We placed them in adjoining rooms, and, as often as was possible, we left the door ajar so that they could call out to one another.

'Poor things! They were little else than boy and girl, and they worried more about each other than they thought about themselves. The wife's only trouble was that she wouldn't be able to do anything for "poor Jack." "Oh, nurse, you will be good to him won't you?" she would cry, with her big childish eyes full of tears; and the moment I went into him it would be: "Oh, don't trouble about me, nurse, I'm all right. Just look after the wifie, will you?"

'I had a hard time between the two of them, for, with the help of her sister, I was nursing them both. It was an unprofessional thing to do, but I could see they were not well off, and I assured the doctor that I could manage. To me it was worth while going through the double work just to breathe the atmosphere of unselfishness that sweetened those two sick-rooms. The average invalid is not the patient sufferer people imagine. It is a fretful, querulous, self-pitying little world that we live in as a rule, and that we grow hard in. It gave me a new heart, nursing these young people.

'The man pulled through, and began steadily to recover, but the wife was a wee slip of a girl, and her strength – what there was of it – ebbed day by day. As he got stronger he would call out more and more cheerfully to her through the open door,

'We left the door ajar so that they could call out to one another'

and ask her how she was getting on, and she would struggle to call back laughing answers. It had been a mistake to put them next to each other, and I blamed myself for having done so, but it was too late to change then. All we could do was to beg her not to exhaust herself, and to let us, when he called out, tell him she was asleep. But the thought of not answering him or calling to him made her so wretched that it seemed safer to let her have her way.

'Her one anxiety was that he should not know how weak she was. "It will worry him so," she would say; "he is such an old fidget over me. And I *am* getting stronger, slowly; ain't I, nurse?"

'One morning he called out to her, as usual, asking her how she was, and she answered, though she had to wait for a few seconds to gather strength to do so. He seemed to detect the effort, for he called back anxiously, "Are you *sure* you're all right, dear?"

'"Yes," she replied, "getting on famously. Why?"

'"I thought your voice sounded a little weak, dear," he answered; "don't call out if it tries you."

'Then for the first time she began to worry about herself – not for her own sake, but because of him.

'"Do you think I *am* getting weaker, nurse?" she asked me, fixing her great eyes on me with a frightened look.

'"You're making yourself weak by calling out," I answered, a little sharply. "I shall have to keep that door shut."

'"Oh, don't tell him" – that was all her thought – "don't let him know it. Tell him I'm strong, won't you, nurse? It will kill him if he thinks I'm not getting well."

'I was glad when her sister came up, and I could get out of the room, for you're not much good at nursing when you feel, as I felt then, as though you had swallowed a tablespoon and it was sticking in your throat.

'Later on, when I went in to him, he drew me to the

'Tell him I'm strong, won't you, nurse?'

bedside, and whispered me to tell him truly how she was. If you are telling a lie at all, you may just as well make it a good one, so I told him she was really wonderfully well, only a little exhausted after the illness, as was natural, and that I expected to have her up before him.

'Poor lad! that lie did him more good than a week's doctoring and nursing; and next morning he called out more cheerily than ever to her, and offered to bet her a new bonnet against a new hat that he would race her, and be up first.

'She laughed back quite merrily (I was in his room at the time). "All right," she said, "you'll lose. I shall be well first, and I shall come and visit you."

'Her laugh was so bright, and her voice sounded so much stronger, that I really began to think she had taken a turn for the better, so that when on going in to her I found her pillow wet with tears, I could not understand it.

'"Why, we were so cheerful just a minute ago," I said; "what's the matter?"

'"Oh, poor Jack!" she moaned, as her little, wasted fingers opened and closed upon the counter-pane. "Poor Jack, it will break his heart."

'It was no good my saying anything. There comes a moment when something tells your patient all that is to be known about the case, and the doctor and the nurse can keep their hopeful assurances for where they will be of more use. The only thing that would have brought comfort to her then would have been to convince her that he would soon forget her and be happy without her. I thought it at the time, and I tried to say something of the kind to her, but I couldn't get it out, and she wouldn't have believed me if I had.

'So all I could do was to go back to the other room, and tell him that I wanted her to go to sleep, and that he must not call out to her until I told him.

'She lay very still all day. The doctor came at his usual hour and looked at her. He patted her hand, and just glanced at the untouched food beside her.

'"Yes," he said, quietly. "I shouldn't worry her, nurse." And I understood.

'Towards evening she opened her eyes, and beckoned to her sister, who was standing by the beside, to bend down.

'"Jeanie," she whispered, "do you think it wrong to deceive any one when it's for their own good?"

'"I don't know," said the girl, in a dry voice; "I shouldn't think so. Why do you ask?"

'"Jeanie, your voice was always very much like mine – do you remember, they used to mistake us at home. Jeanie, call out for me – just till – till he's a bit better; promise me."

'They had loved each other, those two, more than is common among sisters. Jeanie could not answer, but she pressed her sister closer in her arms, and the other was satisfied.

Then, drawing all her little stock of life together for one final effort, the child raised herself in her sister's arms.

'"Good-night, Jack," she called out, loud and clear enough to be heard through the closed door.

'"Good-night, little wife," he cried back, cheerily; "are you all right?"

'I shouldn't worry her, nurse'

'"Yes, dear. Good-night."

'Her little, worn-out frame dropped back upon the bed, and the next thing I remember is snatching up a pillow, and holding it tight-pressed against Jeanie's face for fear the sound of her sobs should penetrate into the next room; and afterwards we both got out, somehow, by the other door, and rushed downstairs, and clung to each other in the back kitchen.

'How we two women managed to keep up the deceit, as, for three whole days, we did, I shall never myself know. Jeanie sat in the room where her dead sister, from its head to its sticking-up feet, lay outlined under the white sheet; and I stayed beside the living man, and told lies and acted lies, till I took a joy in them, and had to guard against the danger of over-elaborating them.

'He wondered at what he thought my "new merry mood," and I told him it was because of my delight that his wife was out of danger; and then I went on for the pure devilment of the thing, and told him that a week ago, when we had let him think his wife was growing stronger, we had been deceiving him; that, as a matter of fact, she was at that time in great peril, and I had been in hourly alarm concerning her, but that now the strain was over, and she was safe; and I dropped down by the foot of the bed, and burst into a fit of laughter, and had to clutch hold of the bedstead to keep myself from rolling on the floor.

'He had started up in bed with a wild white face when Jeanie had first answered him from the other room, though the sisters' voices had been so uncannily alike that I had never been able to distinguish one from the other at any time. I told him the slight change was the result of the fever, that his own voice also was changed a little, and that such was always the case with a person recovering from a long illness. To guide his thoughts away from the real clue, I told him Jeanie had broken down with the long work, and that, the need for her being past, I had packed her off into the country for a short rest. That afternoon we concocted a letter to him, and I watched Jeanie's eyes with a towel in my hand while she wrote it, so that no tears should fall on it, and that night she travelled twenty miles down the Great Western line to post it, returning by the next up-train.

'No suspicion of the truth ever occurred to him, and the doctor helped us out with our deception; yet his pulse, which day by day had been getting stronger, now beat feebler every hour. In that part of the country where I was born and grew up, the folks say that wherever the dead lie, there round about them, whether the time be summer or winter, the air grows cold and colder, and that no fire, though you pile the logs half-way up the chimney, will ever make it warm. A few months' hospital training generally cures one of all fanciful notions about death, but this idea I have never been able to get rid of. My thermometer may show me sixty, and I may try to believe that the temperature *is* sixty, but if the dead are beside me I feel cold to the marrow of my bones. I could *see* the chill from the dead room crawling underneath the door, and creeping up about his bed, and reaching out its hand to touch his heart.

'Jeanie and I redoubled our efforts, for it seemed to us as if Death were waiting just outside in the passage, watching with his eye at the keyhole for either of us to make a blunder and let the truth slip out. I hardly ever left his side except now and again to go into that next room, and poke an imaginary fire, and say a few chaffing words to an imaginary living woman on the bed where the dead one lay; and Jeanie sat close to the corpse, and called out saucy messages to him, or reassuring answers to his anxious questions.

'At times, knowing that if we stopped another moment in these rooms we should scream, we would steal softly out and rush downstairs, and, shutting ourselves out of hearing in a cellar underneath the yard, laugh till we reeled against the dirty walls. I think we were both getting a little mad.

'One day – it was the third of that nightmare life, so I

learned afterwards, though for all I could have told then it might have been the three hundredth, for Time seemed to have fled from that house as from a dream, so that all things were tangled – I made a slip that came near to ending the matter, then and there.

'I had gone into that other room. Jeanie had left her post for a moment, and the place was empty.

'I did not think what I was doing. I had not closed my eyes that I can remember since the wife had died, and my brain and my senses were losing their hold of one another. I went through my usual performance of talking loudly to the thing underneath the white sheet, and noisily patting the pillows and rattling the bottles on the table.

'On my return, he asked me how she was, and I answered, half in a dream, "Oh, bonny, she's trying to read a little," and he raised himself on his elbow and called out to her, and for answer there came back silence – not the silence that *is* silence, but the silence that is as a voice. I do not know if you understand what I mean by that. If you had lived among the dead as long as I have, you would know.

'I darted to the door and pretended to look in. "She's fallen asleep," I whispered, closing it; and he said nothing, but his eyes looked queerly at me.

'That night, Jeanie and I stood in the hall talking. He had fallen asleep early, and I had locked the door between the two rooms, and put the key in my pocket, and had stolen down to tell her what had happened, and to consult with her.

'"What can we do! God help us, what can we do!" was all that Jeanie could say. We had thought that in a day or two he would be stronger, and that the truth might be broken to him. But instead of that he had grown so weak, that to excite his suspicions now by moving him or her would be to kill him.

'We stood looking blankly in each other's faces, wondering how the problem could be solved; and while we did so the problem solved itself.

'The one woman-servant had gone out, and the house was very silent – so silent that I could hear the ticking of Jeanie's watch inside her dress. Suddenly, into the stillness there came a sound. It was not a cry. It came from no human voice. I have heard the voice of human pain till I know its every note, and have grown careless to it; but I have prayed God on my knees that I may never hear that sound again, for it was the sob of a soul.

'It wailed through the quiet house and passed away, and neither of us stirred.

'At length, with the return of the blood to our veins, we went upstairs together He had crept from his own room along the passage into hers. He had not had strength enough to pull the sheet off, though he had tried. He lay across the bed with one hand grasping hers.'

My nurse sat for a while without speaking, a somewhat unusual thing for her to do.

'You ought to write your experiences,' I said.

'Ah!' she said, giving the fire a contemplative poke, 'if you'd seen as much sorrow in the world as I have, you wouldn't want to write a sad book.'

'I think,' she added, after a long pause, with the poker still in her hand, 'it can only be the people who have never *known* suffering who can care to read of it. If I could write a book, I should write a merry book – a book that would make people laugh.'

CHAPTER IX

The discussion arose in this way. I had proposed a match between our villain and the daughter of the local chemist, a singularly noble and pure-minded girl, the humble but worthy friend of the heroine.

Brown had refused his consent on the ground of improbability. 'What in thunder would induce him to marry *her?*' he asked.

'Love!' I replied; 'love, that burns as brightly in the meanest villain's breast as in the proud heart of the good young man.'

'Are you trying to be light and amusing,' returned Brown, severely, 'or are you supposed to be discussing the matter seriously? What attraction could such a girl have for such a man as Reuben Neil?'

'Every attraction,' I retorted. 'She is the exact moral contrast to himself. She is beautiful (if she's not beautiful enough, we can touch her up a bit), and, when the father dies, there will be the shop.'

'Besides,' I added, 'it will make the thing seem more natural if everybody wonders what on earth could have been the reason for their marrying each other.'

Brown wasted no further words on me, but turned to MacShaughnassy.

'Can *you* imagine our friend Reuben seized with a burning desire to marry Mary Holme?' he asked, with a smile.

'Of course I can,' said MacShaughnassy; 'I can imagine anything, and believe anything of anybody. It is only in novels that people act reasonably and in accordance with what might be expected of them. I knew an old sea-captain who used to read the *Young Ladies' Journal* in bed, and cry over it. I knew a bookmaker who always carried Browning's poems about with him in his pocket to study in the train. I have known a Harley Street doctor to develop at forty-eight a sudden and overmastering passion for switchbacks, and to spend every hour he could spare from his practice at one or other of the exhibitions, having three-pen'orths one after the other. I have known a book-reviewer give oranges (not poisoned ones) to children. A man is not a character, he is a dozen characters, one of them prominent, the other eleven more or less undeveloped. I knew a man once, two of whose characters were of equal value, and the consequences were peculiar.'

We begged him to relate the case to us, and he did so.

'He was a Balliol man,' said MacShaughnassy, 'and his Christian name was Joseph. He was a member of the "Devonshire" at the time I knew him, and was, I think, the most superior person I have ever met. He sneered at the *Saturday Review* as the pet journal of the suburban literary club; and at the *Athenaeum* as the trade organ of the unsuccessful writer. Thackeray, he considered, was fairly entitled to his position of favourite author to the cultured clerk; and Carlyle he regarded as the exponent of the earnest artisan. Living authors he never read, but this did not prevent his criticising them contemptuously. The only inhabitants of the nineteenth century that he ever praised were a few obscure French novelists, of whom nobody but himself had ever heard. He had his own opinion

'A *most superior person*'

about God Almighty, and objected to Heaven on account of
the strong Clapham contingent likely to be found in residence
there. Humour made him sad, and sentiment made him ill. Art
irritated him and science bored him. He despised his own
family and disliked everybody else. For exercise he yawned,
and his conversation was mainly confined to an occasional
shrug.

'Nobody liked him, but everybody respected him. One felt
grateful to him for his condescension in living at all.

'One summer, I was fishing over the Norfolk Broads, and on
the Bank Holiday, thinking I would like to see the London
'Arry in his glory, I ran over to Yarmouth. Walking along the
sea-front in the evening, I suddenly found myself confronted
by four remarkably choice specimens of the class. They were
urging on their wild and erratic career arm-in-arm. The one
nearest the road was playing an unusually wheezy concertina,
and the other three were bawling out the chorus of a music-hall
song, the heroine of which appeared to be "Hemmer."

'They spread themselves right across the pavement,

'They spread themselves right
across the pavement'

compelling all the women and children they met to step into the roadway. I stood my ground on the kerb, and as they brushed by me something in the face of the one with the concertina struck me as familiar.

'I turned and followed them. They were evidently enjoying themselves immensely. To every girl they passed they yelled out, "Oh, you little jam tart!" and every old lady they addressed as "Mar." The noisiest and the most vulgar of the four was the one with the concertina.

'I followed them on to the pier, and then, hurrying past, waited for them under a gas-lamp. When the man with the concertina came into the light and I saw him clearly I started. From the face I could have sworn it was Joseph; but everything else about him rendered such an assumption impossible. Putting aside the time and the place, and forgetting his behaviour, his companions, and his instrument, what remained was sufficient to make the suggestion absurd. Joseph was always clean shaven; this youth had a smudgy moustache and a pair of incipient red whiskers. He was dressed in the loudest check suit I have ever seen, off the stage. He wore patent-leather boots with mother-of-pearl buttons, and a neck-tie that in an earlier age would have called down lightning out of Heaven. He had a low-crowned billycock hat on his head, and a big evil-smelling cigar between his lips.

'Argue as I would, however, the face was the face of Joseph; and, moved by a curiosity I could not control, I kept near him, watching him.

'Once, for a little while, I missed him; but there was not much fear of losing that suit for long, and after a little looking about I struck it again. He was sitting at the end of the pier, where it was less crowded, with his arm round a girl's waist. I crept close. She was a jolly, red-faced girl, good-looking enough, but common to the last degree. Her hat lay on the seat beside her, and her head was resting on his shoulder. She appeared to be fond of him, but he was evidently bored.

'"Don'tcher like me, Joe?" I heard her murmur.

'"Yas," he replied, somewhat unconvincingly, "o'course I likes yer."

'She gave him an affectionate slap, but he did not respond, and a few minutes afterwards, muttering some excuse, he rose and left her, and I followed him as he made his way towards the refreshment-room. At the door he met one of his pals.

'"Hullo!" was the question, "wot 'a yer done wi' 'Liza?"

'"Oh, I carn't stand 'er," was his reply; "she gives me the bloomin' 'ump. You 'ave a turn with 'er."

'His friend disappeared in the direction of 'Liza, and Joe pushed into the room, I keeping close behind him. Now that he was alone I was determined to speak to him. The longer I had studied his features the more resemblance I had found in them to those of my superior friend Joseph.

'He was leaning across the bar, clamouring for two of gin, when I tapped him on the shoulder. He turned his head, and the moment he saw me, his face went livid.

'"Mr Joseph Smythe, I believe," I said with a smile.

'"Who's Mr Joseph Smythe?" he answered hoarsely; "my name's Smith, I ain't no bloomin' Smythe. Who are you? I don't know yer."

'As he spoke, my eyes rested upon a curious gold ring of Indian workmanship which he wore upon his left hand. There was no mistaking the ring, at all events: it had been passed round the club on more than one occasion as a unique curiosity. His eyes followed my gaze. He burst into tears, and pushing me before him into a quiet corner of the saloon, sat down facing me.

'"Don't give me away, old man," he whimpered; "for Gawd's sake, don't let on to any of the chaps 'ere that I'm a member of that blessed old waxwork show in Saint James's: they'd never speak to me agen. And keep yer mug shut about Oxford, there's a good sort. I wouldn't 'ave 'em know as 'ow I was one o' them college blokes for anythink."

'I sat aghast. I had listened to hear him entreat me to keep "Smith," the rorty 'Arry, a secret from the acquaintances of "Smythe," the superior person. Here was "Smith" in mortal terror lest his pals should hear of his identity with the aristocratic "Smythe," and discard him. His attitude puzzled me at the time, but, when I came to reflect, my wonder was at myself for having expected the opposite.

'"I carn't 'elp it," he went on; "I 'ave to live two lives. 'Arf my time I'm a stuck-up prig, as orter be jolly well kicked ——"

'"At which times," I interrupted, "I have heard you express some extremely uncomplimentary opinions concerning 'Arries."

'Clamouring for two of gin'

"'I know," he replied, in a voice betraying strong emotion; "that's where it's so precious rough on me. When I'm a toff I despises myself, 'cos I knows that underneath my sneering phiz I'm a bloomin' 'Arry. When I'm an 'Arry, I 'ates myself 'cos I knows I'm a toff."

"'Can't you decide which character you prefer, and stick to it?" I asked.

"'No," he answered, "I carn't. It's a rum thing, but whichever I am, sure as fate, 'bout the end of a month I begin to get sick o' myself."

"'I can quite understand it," I murmured; "I should give way myself in a fortnight."

"'I've been myself, now," he continued, without noticing my remark, "for somethin' like ten days. One mornin', in 'bout three weeks' time, I shall get up in my diggins in the Mile End Road, and I shall look round the room, and at these clothes 'angin' over the bed, and at this yer concertina" (he gave it an affectionate squeeze), "and I shall feel myself gettin' scarlet all over. Then I shall jump out o' bed, and look at myself in the glass. 'You howling little cad,' I shall say to myself, 'I have half a mind to strangle you'; and I shall shave myself, and put on a quiet blue serge suit and a bowler 'at, tell my landlady to keep my rooms for me till I comes back, slip out o' the 'ouse, and into the fust 'ansom I meets, and back to the Halbany. And a month arter that, I shall come into my chambers at the Halbany, fling Voltaire and Parini into the fire, shy me 'at at the bust of good old 'Omer, slip on my blue suit agen, and back to the Mile End Road."

"'How do you explain your absence to both parties?" I asked.

"'Oh, that's simple enough," he replied. "I just tells my 'ousekeeper at the Halbany as I'm goin' on the Continong; and my mates 'ere thinks I'm a traveller."

"'Nobody misses me much," he added, pathetically; "I hain't a partic'larly fetchin' sort o' bloke, either of me. I'm sich an out-and-outer. When I'm an 'Arry, I'm too much of an 'Arry, and when I'm a prig, I'm a reg'lar fust prize prig. Seems to me as if I was two ends of a man without any middle. If I could only mix myself up a bit more, I'd be all right."

'He sniffed once or twice, and then he laughed. "Ah, well," he said, casting aside his momentary gloom; "it's all a game, and wots' the odds so long as yer 'appy. 'Ave a wet?"

'I declined the wet, and left him playing sentimental airs to himself upon the concertina.

'One afternoon, about a month later, the servant came to me with a card on which was engraved the name of "Mr Joseph Smythe." I requested her to show him up. He entered with his usual air of languid superciliousness, and seated himself in a graceful attitude upon the sofa.

'"Well," I said, as soon as the girl had closed the door behind her, "so you've got rid of Smith?"

'A sickly smile passed over his face. "You have not mentioned it to any one?" he asked anxiously.

'"Not to a soul," I replied; "though I confess I often feel tempted to."

'"I sincerely trust you never will," he said, in a tone of alarm. "You can have no conception of the misery the whole thing causes me. I cannot understand it. What possible affinity there can be between myself and that disgusting little snob passes my comprehension. I assure you, my dear Mac, the knowledge that I was a ghoul, or a vampire, would cause me less nausea than the reflection that I am one and the same with that odious little Whitechapel bounder. When I think of him every nerve in my body ——"

'"Don't think about him any more," I interrupted, perceiving his strongly-suppressed emotion. "You didn't come here to talk about him, I'm sure. Let us dismiss him."

'"Well," he replied, "in a certain roundabout way it is slightly connected with him. That is really my excuse for inflicting the subject upon you. You are the only man I *can* speak to about it – if I shall not bore you?"

"'Not in the least,' I said. "I am most interested." As he still hesitated, I asked him point-blank what it was.

'He appeared embarrassed. "It is really very absurd of me," he said, while the faintest suspicion of pink crossed his usually colourless face; "but I feel I must talk to somebody about it. The fact is, my dear Mac, I am in love."

"'Capital!' I cried; "I'm delighted to hear it." (I thought it might make a man of him.) "Do I know the lady?"

"'I am inclined to think you must have seen her," he replied; "she was with me on the pier at Yarmouth that evening you met me."

"'Not 'Liza!' I exclaimed.

"'That was she," he answered; "Miss Elizabeth Muggins." He dwelt lovingly upon the name.

"'But," I said, "you seemed – I really could not help noticing, it was so pronounced – you seemed to positively dislike her. Indeed, I gathered from your remark to a friend that her society was distinctly distasteful to you."

"'To Smith," he corrected me. "What judge would that howling little blackguard be of a woman's worth! The dislike of such a man as that is a testimonial to her merit!"

"'I may be mistaken," I said; "but she struck me as a bit common."

"'She is not, perhaps, what the world would call a lady," he admitted; "but then, my dear Mac, my opinion of the world is not such as to render *its* opinion of much value to me. I and the world differ on most subjects, I am glad to say. She is beautiful, and she is good, and she is my choice."

"'She's a jolly enough little girl," I replied, "and, I should say, affectionate; but have you considered, Smythe, whether she is quite – what shall we say – quite as intellectual as could be desired?"

"'Really, to tell the truth, I have not troubled myself much about her intellect," he replied, with one of his sneering smiles. "I have no doubt that the amount of intellect absolutely necessary to the formation of a British home, I shall be able to supply myself. I have no desire for an intellectual wife. One is compelled to meet tiresome people, but one does not live with them if one can avoid it."

'"No," he continued, reverting to his more natural tone; "the more I think of Elizabeth the more clear it becomes to me that she is the one woman in the world for whom marriage with me is possible. I perceive that to the superficial observer my selection must appear extraordinary. I do not pretend to explain it, or even to understand it. The study of mankind is beyond man. Only fools attempt it. Maybe it is her contrast to myself that attracts me. Maybe my, perhaps, too spiritual

'I came across her in an aerated bread shop'

nature feels the need of contact with her coarser clay to perfect itself. I cannot tell. These things must always remain mysteries. I only know that I love her – that, if any reliance is to be placed upon instinct, she is the mate to whom Artemis is leading me."

'It was clear that he was in love, and I therefore ceased to argue with him. "You kept up your acquaintanceship with her, then after you" – I was going to say "after you ceased to be Smith," but not wishing to agitate him by more mention of that person than I could help, I substituted, "after you returned to the Albany?"

'"Not exactly," he replied; "I lost sight of her after I left Yarmouth, and I did not see her again until five days ago, when I came across her in an aerated bread shop. I had gone in to get a glass of milk and a bun, and *she* brought them to me. I recognised her in a moment." His face lighted up with quite a human smile. "I take tea there every afternoon now," he added, glancing towards the clock, "at four."

'"There's not much need to ask *her* views on the subject," I said, laughing; "her feelings towards you were pretty evident."

'"Well, that is the curious part of it," he replied, with a return to his former embarrassment; "she does not seem to care for me now at all. Indeed, she positively refuses me. She says – to put it in the dear child's own racy language – that she wouldn't take me on at any price. She says it would be like marrying a clockwork figure without the key. She's more frank than complimentary, but I like that."

'"Wait a minute," I said; "an idea occurs to me. Does she know of your identity with Smith?"

'"No," he replied, alarmed, "I would not have her know it for worlds. Only yesterday she told me that I reminded her of a fellow she had met at Yarmouth, and my heart was in my mouth."

'"How did she look when she told you that?" I asked.

'"How did she look?" he repeated, not understanding me.

'"What was her expression at that moment?" I said – "was it severe or tender?"

'"Well," he replied, "now I come to think of it, she did seem to soften a bit just then."

'"My dear boy," I said, "the case is as clear as daylight. She loved Smith. No girl who admired Smith could be attracted by Smythe. As your present self you will never win her. In a few weeks' time, however, you will be Smith. Leave the matter over until then. Propose to her as Smith, and she will accept you. After marriage you can break Smythe gently to her."

'"By Jove!" he exclaimed, startled out of his customary lethargy, "I never thought of that. The truth is, when I am in my right sense, Smith and all his affairs seem like a dream to me. Any idea connected with him would never enter my mind."

'He rose and held out his hand. "I am so glad I came to see you," he said; "your suggestion has almost reconciled me to my miserable fate. Indeed, I quite look forward to a month of Smith, now."

'"I'm so pleased," I answered, shaking hands with him. "Mind you come and tell me how you get on. Another man's love affairs are not usually absorbing, but there is an element of interest about yours that renders the case exceptional."

'We parted, and I did not see him again for another month. Then, late one evening, the servant knocked at my door to say that a Mr Smith wished to see me.

'"Smith, Smith," I repeated; "what Smith? didn't he give you a card?"

'"No, sir," answered the girl; "he doesn't look the sort that would have a card. He's not a gentleman, sir; but he says you'll know him." She evidently regarded the statement as an aspersion upon myself.

'I was about to tell her to say I was out, when the recollection of Smythe's other self flashed into my mind, and I directed her to send him up.

'A minute passed, and then he entered. He was wearing a new suit of a louder pattern, if possible, than before. I think he must have designed it himself. He looked hot and greasy. He did not offer to shake hands, but sat down awkwardly on the extreme edge of a small chair, and gaped about the room as if he had never seen it before.

'He communicated his shyness to myself. I could not think what to say, and we sat for a while in painful silence.

'"Well," I said, at last, plunging head-foremost into the matter, according to the method of shy people, "and how's 'Liza?"

'"Oh, *she's* all right," he replied, keeping his eyes fixed on his hat.

'"Have you done it?" I continued.

'"Done wot?" he asked, looking up.

'"Married her."

'"No," he answered, returning to the contemplation of his hat.

'"Has she refused you then?" I said.

'"I ain't arst 'er," he returned.

He seemed unwilling to explain matters of his own accord. I had to put the conversation into the form of a cross-examination.

'"Why not?" I asked; "don't you think she cares for you any longer?"

He burst into a harsh laugh. "There ain't much fear o' that," he said; "it's like 'aving an Alcock's porous plaster mashed on yer, blowed if it ain't. There's no gettin' rid of 'er. I wish she'd giv' somebody else a turn. I'm fair sick of 'er."

'"But you were enthusiastic about her a month ago!" I exclaimed in astonishment.

'"Smythe may 'ave been," he said; "there ain't no accounting for that ninny, 'is 'ead's full of starch. Anyhow, I don't take 'er on while I'm myself. I'm too jolly fly."

'"That sort o' gal's all right enough to lark with," he

continued; "but yer don't want to marry 'em. They don't do yer no good. A man wants a wife as 'e can respect – some one as is a cut above 'imself, as will raise 'im up a peg or two – some one as 'e can look up to and worship. A man's wife orter be to 'im a gawddess – a hangel, a——"

'"You appear to have met the lady," I remarked, interrupting him.

'He blushed scarlet, and became suddenly absorbed in the pattern of the carpet. But the next moment he looked up again, and his face seemed literally transformed.

'"Oh! Mr MacShaughnassy," he burst out, with a ring of genuine manliness in his voice, "you don't know 'ow good, 'ow beautiful she is. I ain't fit to breathe 'er name in my thoughts.

'Opened the carriage door for 'er'

An' she's so clever. I met 'er at that Toynbee 'All. There was a party of toffs there all together. You would 'ave enjoyed it, Mr MacShaughnassy, if you could 'ave 'eard 'er; she was makin' fun of the pictures and the people round about to 'er pa – such wit, such learnin', such 'aughtiness. I follered them out and opened the carriage door for 'er, and she just drew 'er skirt aside and looked at me as if I was the dirt in the road. I wish I was, for then perhaps one day I'd kiss 'er feet."

'His emotion was so genuine that I did not feel inclined to laugh at him. "Did you find out who she was?" I asked.

'"Yes," he answered; "I 'eard the old gentleman say ''Ome' to the coachman, and I ran after the carriage all the say to 'Arley Street. Trevior's 'er name, Hedith Trevior."

'"Miss Trevior!" I cried, "a tall, dark girl, with untidy hair and rather weak eyes?"

'"Tall and dark," he replied; "with 'air that seems tryin' to reach 'er lips to kiss 'em, and heyes, light blue, like a Cambridge necktie. A 'undred and seventy-three was the number."

'"That's right," I said; "my dear Smith, this is becoming complicated. You've met the lady and talked to her for half an hour – as Smythe, don't you remember?"

'"No." he said, after cogitating for a minute, "carn't say I do; I never can remember much about Smythe. He allers seems to me like a bad dream."

'"Well, you met her," I said; "I'm positive. I introduced you to her myself, and she confided to me afterwards that she thought you a most charming man."

'"No – did she?" he remarked, evidently softening in his feelings towards Smythe; 'and did *I* like 'er?"

'"Well, to tell the truth," I answered, 'I don't think you did. You looked intensely bored."

'"The Juggins," I heard him mutter to himself, and then he said aloud: "D'yer think I shall get a chance o' seein' 'er agen, when I'm – when I'm Smythe?"

'"Of course," I said, "I'll take you round myself. By the bye," I added, jumping up and looking on the mantelpiece, "I've got a card for a Cinderella at their place – something to do with a birthday. Will you be Smythe on November the twentieth?'

'"Ye – as," he replied; "oh, yas – bound to be by then."

'"Very well, then," I said, "I'll call round for you at the Albany, and we'll go together."

'He rose and stood smoothing his hat with his sleeve. "Fust time I've ever looked for'ard to bein' that hanimated corpse, Smythe," he said slowly. "Blowed if I don't try to 'urry it up – 'pon my sivey I will."

'"He'll be no good to you till the twentieth," I reminded him. "And," I added, as I stood up to ring the bell, "you're sure it's a genuine case this time. You won't be going back to 'Liza?"

'"Oh, don't talk 'bout 'Liza in the same breath with Hedith," he replied, "it sounds like sacrilege."

'He stood hesitating with the handle of the door in his hand. At last, opening it and looking very hard at his hat, he said, '"I'm goin' to 'Arley Street now. I walk up and down outside the 'ouse every evening, and sometimes, when there ain't no one lookin', I get a chance to kiss the doorstep."

'He disappeared, and I returned to my chair.

'On November twentieth, I called for him according to promise. I found him on the point of starting for the club: he had forgotten all about our appointment. I reminded him of it, and he with difficulty recalled it, and consented, without any enthusiasm, to accompany me. By a few artful hints to her mother (including a casual mention of his income), I manoeuvred matters so that he had Edith almost entirely to himself for the whole evening. I was proud of what I had done, and as we were walking home together I waited to received his gratitude.

'As it seemed slow in coming, I hinted my expectations.

'"Well," I said, "I think I managed that very cleverly for you."

"'Managed what very cleverly?" said he.

"'Why, getting you and Miss Trevior left together for such a long time in the conservatory," I answered, some what hurt; "*I* fixed that for you."

"'Oh, it was *you*, was it," he replied; "I've been cursing Providence."

'I stopped dead in the middle of the pavement, and faced him. "Don't you love her?" I said.

"'Love her!' he repeated, in the utmost astonishment; "what on earth is there in her to love? She's nothing but a bad translation of a modern French comedy, with the interest omitted."

'This "tired" me – to use an Americanism. "You came to me

'What on earth is there in her to love?'

a month ago," I said, "raving over her, and talking about being the dirt under her feet and kissing her doorstep."

'He turned very red. "I wish, my dear Mac," he said, "you would pay me the compliment of not mistaking me for that detestable little cad with whom I have the misfortune to be connected. You would greatly oblige me if next time he attempts to inflict upon you his vulgar drivel you would kindly kick him downstairs.'

'"No doubt," he added, with a sneer, as we walked on, "Miss Trevior would be his ideal. She is exactly the type of women, I should say, to charm that type of man. For myself, I do not appreciate the artistic and literary female."

'"Besides," he continued, in a deeper tone, "you know my feelings. I shall never care for any other woman but Elizabeth."

'"And she?" I said ——

'"She," he sighed, "is breaking her heart for Smith."

'"Why don't you tell her you are Smith?" I asked.

'"I cannot," he replied, "not even to win her. Besides, she would not believe me."

'We said good-night at the corner of Bond Street, and I did not see him again till one afternoon late in the following March, when I ran against him in Ludgate Circus. He was wearing his transition blue suit and bowler hat. I went up to him and took his arm.

'"Which are you?" I said.

'"Neither, for the moment," he replied, "thank God. Half an hour ago I was Smythe, half an hour hence I shall be Smith. For the present half-hour I am a man."

'There was a pleasant, hearty ring in his voice, and a genial, kindly light in his eyes, and he held himself like a frank gentleman.

'"You are certainly an improvement upon both of them," I said.

'He laughed a sunny laugh, with just the shadow of sadness dashed across it. "Do you know my idea of Heaven?" he said.

'"No," I replied, somewhat surprised at the question.

'"Ludgate Circus," was the answer. "The only really satisfying moments of my life," he said, "have been passed in the neighbourhood of Ludgate Circus. I leave Piccadilly an unhealthy, unwholesome prig. At Charing Cross I began to feel my blood stir in my veins. From Ludgate Circus to Cheapside I am a human thing with human feeling throbbing in my heart, and human thought throbbing in my brain – with fancies, sympathies, and hopes. At the Bank my mind becomes a blank. As I walk on, my senses grow coarse and blunted; and by the time I reach Whitechapel I am a poor little uncivilised cad. On the return journey it is the same thing reversed."

'"Why not live in Ludgate Circus," I said, "and be always as you are now?"

'"Because," he answered, "man is a pendulum, and must travel his arc."

'"My dear Mac," said he, laying his hand upon my shoulder, "there is only one good thing about me, and that is a moral. Man is as God made him: don't be so sure that you can take him to pieces and improve him. All my life I have sought to make myself an unnaturally superior person. Nature has retaliated by making me also an unnaturally inferior person. Nature abhors lopsidedness. She turns out man as a whole, to be developed as a whole. I always wonder, whenever I come across a supernaturally pious, a supernaturally moral, a supernaturally cultured person, if they also have a reverse self."

'I was shocked at his suggested argument, and walked by his side for a while without speaking. At last, feeling curious on the subject, I asked him how his various love affairs were progressing.

'"Oh, as usual," he replied; "in and out of a *cul de sac*. When I am Smythe I love Eliza, and Eliza loathes me. When I am Smith I love Edith, and the mere sight of me makes her shudder. It is as unfortunate for them as for me. I am not saying it boastfully. Heaven knows it is an added draught of misery in my cup; but it is a fact that Eliza is literally pining away for me as Smith, and as Smith I find it impossible to be even civil to her; while Edith, poor girl, has been foolish enough to set her heart on me as Smythe, and as Smythe she seems to me but the skin of a woman stuffed with the husks of learning, and rags torn from the corpse of wit."

'I remained absorbed in my own thoughts for some time, and did not come out of them till we were crossing the Minories. Then, the idea suddenly occurring to me, I said:

'"Why don't you get a new girl altogether? There must be medium girls that both Smith and Smythe could like, and that would put up with both of you."

'"No more girls for this child," he answered; "they're more trouble than they're worth. Those yer want yer carn't get, and those yer can 'ave, yer don't want."

'I started, and looked up at him. He was slouching along with his hands in his pockets, and a vacuous look in his face.

'A sudden repulsion seized me. "I must go now," I said, stopping. "I'd no idea I had come so far."

'He seemed as glad to be rid of me as I to be rid of him. "Oh, must yer," he said, holding out his hand. "Well, so long."

'We shook hands carelessly. He disappeared in the crowd, and that is the last I have ever seen of him.'

'Is that a true story?' asked Jephson.

'Well, I've altered the names and dates,' said MacShaughnassy; 'but the main facts you can rely upon.'

CHAPTER X

The final question discussed at our last meeting had been:
What shall our hero be? MacShaughnassy had suggested an
author, with a critic for the villain. My idea was a stockbroker,
with an undercurrent of romance in his nature. Said Jephson,
who has a practical mind: 'the question is not what we like, but
what the female novel-reader likes.'

'That is so,' agreed MacShaughnassy. 'I propose that we
collect feminine opinion upon this point. I will write to my

aunt and obtain from her the old lady's view. You,' he said, turning to me, 'can put the case to your wife, and get the young lady's ideal. Let Brown write to his sister at Newnham, and find out whom the intellectual maiden favours, while Jephson can learn from Miss Medbury what is most attractive to the common-sensed girl.'

This plan we had adopted, and the result was now under consideration. MacShaughnassy opened the proceedings by reading his aunt's letter. Wrote the old lady:

'I think, if I were you, my dear boy, I should choose a soldier. You know your poor grandfather, who ran away to America with that *wicked* Mrs Featherly, the banker's wife, was a soldier, and so was your poor cousin Robert, who lost eight thousand pounds at Monte Carlo. I have always felt singularly drawn towards soldiers, even as a girl; though your poor dear uncle could not bear them. You will find many allusions to soldiers and men of war in the Old Testament (see Jer. xlviii. 14). Of course one does not like to think of their fighting and killing each other, but then they do not seem to do that sort of thing nowadays.'

'So much for the old lady,' said MacShaughnassy, as he folded up the letter and returned it to his pocket. 'What says culture?'

Brown produced from his cigar-case a letter addressed in a bold round hand, and read as follows:

'What a curious coincidence! A few of us were discussing this very subject last night in Millicent Hightopper's rooms, and I may tell you at once that our decision was unanimous in favour of soldiers. You see, my dear Selkirk, in human nature the attraction is towards the opposite. To a milliner's apprentice a poet would no doubt be satisfying; to a woman of intelligence he would be an unutterable bore. What the intellectual woman requires in man is not something to argue with, but something to look at. To an empty-headed woman I can imagine the soldier type proving vapid and uninteresting; to the woman of mind he represents her ideal of man – a creature strong, handsome, well-dressed, and not too clever.'

'That give us two votes for the army,' remarked MacShaughnassy, as Brown tore his sister's letter in two, and threw the pieces into the waste-paper basket. 'What says the common-sensed girl?'

'First catch your common-sensed girl,' muttered Jephson, a little grumpily, as it seemed to me. 'Where do you propose finding her?'

'Well,' returned MacShaughnassy, 'I looked to find her in Miss Medbury.'

As a rule, the mention of Miss Medbury's name brings a flush of joy to Jephson's face; but now his feature wore an expression distinctly approaching a scowl.

'Oh!' he replied, 'did you? Well, then, the common-sensed girl loves the military also.'

'By Jove!' exclaimed MacShaughnassy, 'what an extraordinary thing. What reason does she give?'

'That there's a something about them, and that they dance so divinely,' answered Jephson, shortly.

'Well, you do surprise me,' murmured MacShaughnassy, 'I am astonished.'

Then to me he said: 'And what does the young married woman say? The same?'

'Yes,' I replied, 'precisely the same.'

'Does *she* give a reason?' he asked.

'Oh yes,' I explained; 'because you can't help liking them.'

There was silence for the next few minutes, while we smoked and thought. I fancy we were all wishing we had never started this inquiry.

That four distinctly different types of educated womanhood

should, with promptness and unanimity quite unfeminine, have selected the soldier as their ideal, was certainly discouraging to the civilian heart. Had they been nursemaids or servant girls, I should have expected it. The worship of Mars by the Venus of the white cap is one of the few vital religions left to this devoutless age. A year or two ago I lodged near a barracks, and the sight to be seen around its huge iron gates on Sunday afternoons I shall never forget. The girls began to assemble about twelve o'clock. By two, at which hour the army, with its hair nicely oiled and a cane in its hand, was ready for a stroll, there would be some four or five hundred of them waiting in a line. Formerly they had collected in a wild mob, and as the soldiers were let out to them two at a time, had fought for them, as lions for early Christians. This, however, had led to scenes of such disorder and brutality, that the police had been obliged to interfere; and the girls were now marshalled in *queue*, two abreast, and compelled, by a force of constables specially told off for the purpose, to keep their places and wait their proper turn.

At three o'clock the sentry on duty would come down to the wicket and close it. 'They're all gone, my dears,' he would shout out to the girls still left; 'it's no good your stopping, we've no more for you to-day.'

'Oh, not one!' some poor child would murmur pleadingly, while the tears welled up into her big round eye, 'not even a little one. I've been waiting *such* a long time.'

'Can't help that,' the honest fellow would reply, gruffly, but not unkindly, turning aside to hide his emotion; 'you've had 'em all between you. We don't make 'em, you know: you can't have 'em if we haven't got 'em, can you? Come earlier next time.'

Then he would hurry away to escape further importunity; and the police, who appeared to have been waiting for this moment with gloating anticipation, would jeeringly hustle away the weeping remnant. 'Now then, pass along, you girls, pass along,' they would say, in that irritatingly unsympathetic voice of theirs. 'You've had your chance. Can't have the roadway blocked up all the afternoon with this 'ere demonstration of the unloved. Pass along.'

In connection with this same barracks, our charwoman told Amenda, who told Ethelbertha, who told me a story, which I now told the boys.

Into a certain house, in a certain street in the neighbourhood, there moved one day a certain family. Their servant had left them – most of their servants did at the end of a week – and the day after the moving-in an advertisement for a domestic was drawn up and sent to the *Chronicle*. It ran thus:

WANTED, GENERAL SERVANT, in small family of eleven. Wages, £6; no beer money. Must be early riser and hard worker. Washing done at home. Must be good cook, and not object to window-cleaning. Unitarian preferred. – Apply, with references, to A. B., etc.

That advertisement was sent off on Wednesday afternoon. At seven o'clock on Thursday morning the whole family were awakened by continuous ringing of the street-door bell. The husband, looking out of window, was surprised to see a crowd of about fifty girls surrounding the house. He slipped on his dressing-gown and went down to see what was the matter. The moment he opened the door, fifteen of them charged tumultuously into the passage, sweeping him completely off his legs. Once inside, these fifteen faced round, fought the other thirty-five or so back on to the door-step, and slammed the door in their faces. Then they picked up the master of the house, and asked him politely to conduct them to 'A. B.'

At first, owing to the clamour of the mob outside, who were hammering at the door and shouting curses through the keyhole, he could understand nothing, but at length they succeeded in explaining to him that they were domestic

servants come in answer to his wife's advertisement. The man
went and told his wife, and his wife said she would see them,
one at a time.

Which one should have audience first was a delicate question
to decide. The man, on being appealed to, said he would prefer
to leave it to them. They accordingly discussed the matter
among themselves. At the end of a quarter of an hour, the
victor, having borrowed some hair-pins and a looking-glass
from our charwoman, who had slept in the house, went
upstairs, while the remaining fourteen sat down in the hall,
and fanned themselves with their bonnets.

'A. B.' was a good deal astonished when the first applicant
presented herself. She was a tall, genteel-looking girl. Up to
yesterday she had been head housemaid at Lady Stanton's, and
before that she had been under-cook for two years to the
Duchess of York.

'And why did you leave Lady Stanton?' asked 'A. B.'

'To come here, mum,' replied the girl.

The lady was puzzled.

'And you'll be satisfied with six pounds a year?' she asked.

'Certainly, mum, I think it ample.'

'And you don't mind hard work?'

'I love it, mum.'

'And you're an early riser?'

'Oh yes, mum, it upsets me stopping in bed after half-past
five.'

'You know we do the washing at home?'

'Yes, mum. I think it so much better to do it at home. Those
laundries ruin good clothes. They're so careless.'

'Are you a Unitarian?' continued the lady.

'Not yet, mum,' replied the girl, 'but I should like to be one.'

The lady took her reference, and said she would write.

The next applicant offered to come for three pounds –
thought six pounds too much. She expressed her willingness to
sleep in the back kitchen: a shakedown under the sink was all

she wanted. She likewise had yearnings towards Unitarianism.

The third girl did not require any wages at all – could not understand what servants wanted with wages – thought wages only encouraged a love of foolish finery – thought a comfortable home in a Unitarian family ought to be sufficient wages for any girl.

This girl said there was one stipulation she should like to make, and that was that she should be allowed to pay for all breakages caused by her own carelessness or neglect. She objected to holidays and evenings out; she held that they distracted a girl from her work.

The fourth candidate offered a premium of five pounds for the place; and then 'A. B.' began to get frightened, and refused to see any more of the girls, convinced that they must be lunatics from some neighbouring asylum out for a walk.

Later in the day, meeting the next-door lady on the door-step, she related her morning's experiences.

'Oh, that's nothing extraordinary,' said the next-door lady; 'none of us on this side of the street pay wages; and we get the pick of all the best servants in London. Why, girls will come from the other end of the kingdom to get into one of these houses. It's the dream of their lives. They save up for years, so as to be able to come here for nothing.'

'What's the attraction?' asked 'A. B.,' more amazed than ever.

Met the next-door neighbour on the door-step

'Why, don't you see,' explained the next-door lady, 'our back windows open upon the barrack yard. A girl living in one of these houses is always close to soldiers. By looking out of window she can always see soldiers; and sometimes a soldier will nod to her or even call up to her. They never dream of asking for wages. They'll work eighteen hours a day, and put up with anything just to be allowed to stop.'

'A. B.' profited by this information, and engaged the girl who offered the five pounds premium. She found her a perfect treasure of a servant. She was invariably willing and respectful, slept on a sofa in the kitchen, and was always contented with an egg for her dinner.

The truth of this story I cannot vouch for. Myself I can believe it. Brown and MacShaughnassy made no attempt to do so, which seemed unfriendly. Jephson excused himself on the plea of a headache. I admit there are points in it presenting difficulties to the average intellect. As I explained at the commencement, it was told to me by Ethelbertha, who had it from Amenda, who got it from the charwoman, and the exaggerations may have crept into it. The following, however, were incidents that came under my own personal observation. They afforded a still stronger example of the influence exercised by Tommy Atkins upon the British domestic, and I therefore thought it right to relate them.

'The heroine of them,' I said, 'is our Amenda. Now, you would call her a tolerably well-behaved, orderly young woman, would you not?'

'She is my ideal of unostentatious respectability,' answered MacShaughnassy.

'That was my opinion also,' I replied. 'You can, therefore, imagine my feelings on passing her one evening in the Folkestone High Street with a Panama hat upon her head (*my* Panama hat), and a soldier's arm round her waist. She was one of a mob following the band of the Third Berkshire Infantry, then in camp at Sandgate. There was an ecstatic, far-away look in her eyes. She was dancing rather than walking, and with her left hand she beat time to the music.

'Ethelbertha was with me at the time. We stared after the procession until it had turned the corner, and then we stared at each other.

'"Oh, it's impossible," said Ethelbertha to me.

'"But that was my hat," I said to Ethelbertha.

'The moment we reached home Ethelbertha looked for Amenda, and I looked for my hat. Neither was to be found.

'Nine o'clock struck, ten o'clock struck. At half-past ten, we went down and got our own supper, and had it in the kitchen. At a quarter-past eleven, Amenda returned. She walked into the kitchen without a word, hung my hat up behind the door, and commenced clearing away the supper things.

'Ethelbertha rose, calm but severe.

'"Where have you been, Amenda?" she inquired.

'"Gadding half over the county with a lot of low soldiers," answered Amenda, continuing her work.

'"You had on my hat," I added.

'"Yes, sir," replied Amenda, still continuing her work, "it was the first thing that came to hand. What I'm thankful for is that it wasn't missis's best bonnet."

'Whether Ethelbertha was mollified by the proper spirit displayed in this last remark, I cannot say, but I think it probable. At all events, it was in a voice more of sorrow than of anger that she resumed her examination.

'"You were walking with a soldier's arm around your waist when we passed you, Amenda?" she observed interrogatively.

'"I know, mum," admitted Amenda, "I found it there myself when the music stopped."

'Ethelbertha looked her inquiries. Amenda filled a saucepan with water, and then replied to them.

'"I'm a disgrace to a decent household," she said; "no mistress who respected herself would keep me a moment. I ought to be put on the doorstep with my box and a month's wages."

'"But why did you do it then?" said Ethelbertha, with natural astonishment.

'"Because I'm a helpless ninny, mum. I can't help myself; if I see soldiers I'm bound to follow them. It runs in our family. My poor cousin Emma was just such another fool. She was engaged to be married to a quiet, respectable young fellow with a shop of his own, and three days before the wedding she ran off with a regiment of marines to Chatham and married the colour-sergeant. That's what I shall end by doing. I've been all the way to Sandgate with that lot you saw me with, and I've kissed four of them – the nasty wretches. I'm a nice sort of girl to be walking out with a respectable milkman."

'She was so deeply disgusted with herself that it seemed superfluous for anybody else to be indignant with her; and Ethelbertha changed her tone and tried to comfort her.

'"Oh, you'll get over all that nonsense, Amenda," she said, laughingly; "you see yourself how silly it is. You must tell Mr Bowles to keep you away from soldiers."

'"Ah, I can't look at it in the same light way that you do, mum," returned Amenda, somewhat reprovingly; "a girl that can't see a bit of red marching down the street without wanting to rush out and follow it ain't fit to be anybody's wife. Why, I should be leaving the shop with nobody in it about twice a week, and he'd have to go the round of all the barracks in London, looking for me. I shall save up and get myself into a lunatic asylum, that's what I shall do."

'Ethelbertha began to grow quite troubled. "But surely this is something altogether new, Amenda," she said; "you must have often met soldiers when you've been out in London?"

'"Oh yes, one or two at a time, walking about anyhow, I can stand that all right. It's when there's a lot of them with a band that I lose my head."

'"You don't know what it's like, mum," she added, noticing Ethelbertha's puzzled expression; "you've never had it. I only hope you never may."

'We kept a careful watch over Amenda during the remainder of our stay at Folkestone, and an anxious time we had of it. Every day some regiment or other would march through the town, and at the first sound of its music Amenda would become restless and excited. The Pied Piper's reed could not have stirred the Hamelin children deeper than did those Sandgate bands the heart of our domestic. Fortunately, they generally passed early in the morning when we were indoors, but one day, returning home to lunch, we heard distant strains dying away upon the Hythe Road. We hurried in. Ethelbertha ran down into the kitchen; it was empty! – up into Amenda's bedroom; it was vacant! We called. There was no answer.

'"That miserable girl has gone off again," said Ethelbertha. "What a terrible misfortune it is for her. It's quite a disease."

'Ethelbertha wanted me to go to Sandgate camp and inquire for her. I was sorry for the girl myself, but the picture of a young and innocent-looking man wandering about a complicated camp, inquiring for a lost domestic, presenting itself to my mind, I said that I'd rather not.

'Ethelbertha thought me heartless, and said that if I would not go she would go herself. I replied that I thought one female member of my household was enough in that camp at a time, and requested her not to. Ethelbertha expressed her sense of my inhuman behaviour by haughtily declining to eat any lunch, and I expressed my sense of her unreasonableness by sweeping the whole meal into the grate, after which Ethelbertha suddenly developed exuberant affection for the cat (who didn't want anybody's love, but wanted to get under the grate after the lunch), and I became supernaturally absorbed in the day-before-yesterday's newspaper.

'In the afternoon, strolling out into the garden, I heard the faint cry of a female in distress. I listened attentively, and the cry was repeated. I thought it sounded like Amenda's voice, but where it came from I could not conceive. It drew nearer, however, as I approached the bottom of the garden, and at last

I located it in a small wooden shed, used by the proprietor of the house as a dark-room for developing photographs.

'The door was locked. "Is that you, Amenda?" I cried through the keyhole.

'"Yes, sir," came back the muffled answer. "Will you please let me out? you'll find the key on the ground near the door."

'I discovered it on the grass about a yard away, and released her. "Who locked you in?" I asked.

'"I did, sir," she replied; "I locked myself in, and pushed the key out under the door. I had to do it, or I should have gone off with those beastly soldiers."

'"I hope I haven't inconvenienced you, sir," she added, stepping out; "I left the lunch all laid."'

'Who locked you in there?'

Amenda's passion for soldiers was her one tribute to sentiment. Towards all others of the male sex she maintained an attitude of callous unsusceptibility, and her engagements with them (which were numerous) were entered in or abandoned on grounds so sordid as to seriously shock Ethelbertha.

When she came to us she was engaged to a pork butcher – with a milkman in reserve. For Amenda's sake we dealt with the man, but we never liked him, and we liked his pork still less. When, therefore, Amenda announced to us that her engagement with him was 'off,' and intimated that her feelings would in no way suffer by our going elsewhere for our bacon, we secretly rejoiced.

'I am confident you have done right, Amenda,' said Ethelbertha; 'you would never have been happy with that man.'

'No, mum, I don't think I ever should,' replied Amenda. 'I don't see how any girl could as hadn't the digestion of an ostrich.'

Ethelbertha looked puzzled. 'But what has digestion got to do with it?' she asked.

'A pretty good deal, mum,' answered Amenda, 'when you're thinking of marrying a man as can't make a sausage fit to eat.'

'But surely,' exclaimed Ethelbertha, 'you don't mean to say you're breaking off the match because you don't like his sausages!'

'Well, I suppose that's what it comes to,' agreed Amenda, unconcernedly.

'What an awful idea!' sighed poor Ethelbertha, after a long pause. 'Do you think you ever really loved him?'

'Oh yes,' said Amenda, 'I loved him right enough, but it's no good loving a man that wants you to live on sausages that keep you awake all night.'

'But does he want you to live on sausages?' persisted Ethelbertha.

'Oh, he doesn't say anything about it,' explained Amenda; 'but you know what it is mum, when you marry a pork butcher; you're expected to eat what's left over. That's the

Her engagement was 'off'

mistake my poor cousin Eliza made. She married a muffin man. Of course, what he didn't sell they had to finish up themselves. Why, one winter, when he had a run of bad luck, they lived for two months on nothing but muffins. I never saw a girl so changed in all my life. One has to think of these things, you know.'

Gave her a cocoanut

But the most shamefully mercenary engagement that I think Amenda ever entered into, was one with a 'bus conductor. We were living in the north of London then, and she had a young man, a cheesemonger, who kept a shop in Lupus Street, Chelsea. He could not come up to her because of the shop, so once a week she used to go down to him. One did not ride ten miles for a penny in those days, and she found the fare from Holloway to Victoria and back a severe tax upon her purse. The same 'bus that took her down at six brought her back at ten. During the first journey the 'bus conductor stared at Amenda; during the second he talked to her, during the third he gave her a cocoanut, during the fourth he proposed to her, and was promptly accepted. After that, Amenda was enabled to visit her cheesemonger without expense.

He was a quaint character himself, this 'bus conductor. I often rode with him to Fleet Street. He knew me quite well (I suppose Amenda must have pointed me out to him), and would always ask me after her – aloud, before all the other passengers, which was trying – and give me messages to take back to her. Where women were concerned he had what is called 'a way' with him, and from the extent and variety of his female acquaintance, and the evident tenderness with which the majority of them regarded him, I am inclined to hope that Amenda's desertion of him (which happened contemporaneously with her jilting of the cheesemonger) caused him less prolonged suffering than might otherwise have been the case.

He was a man from whom I derived a good deal of amusement one way and another. Thinking of him brings back to my mind a somewhat odd incident.

One afternoon, I jumped upon his 'bus in the Seven Sisters Road. An elderly Frenchman was the only other occupant of the vehicle. 'You vil not forget me,' the Frenchman was saying as I entered, 'I desire Sharing Cross.'

'I won't forget yer,' answered the conductor, 'you shall 'ave yer Sharing Cross. Don't make a fuss about it.'

'That's the third time 'ee's arst me not to forget 'im,' he remarked to me in a stentorian aside; ''ee don't giv' yer much chance of doin' it, does 'ee?'

At the corner of the Holloway Road we drew up, and our conductor began to shout after the manner of his species: 'Charing Cross – Charing Cross – 'ere yer are – Come along, lady – Charing Cross.'

The little Frenchman jumped up, and prepared to exit; the conductor pushed him back.

'Sit down and don't be silly,' he said; 'this ain't Charing Cross.'

The Frenchman looked puzzled, but collapsed meekly. We picked up a few passengers, and proceeded on our way. Half a mile up the Liverpool Road a lady stood on the kerb regarding us as we passed with that pathetic mingling of desire and distrust which is the average woman's attitude towards conveyances of all kinds. Our conductor stopped.

'Where d'yer want to go to?' he asked her severely – 'Strand – Charing Cross?'

The Frenchman did not hear or did not understand the first part of the speech, but he caught the words 'Charing Cross,' and bounced up and out on to the step. The conductor collared him as he was getting off, and jerked him back savagely.

'Carn't yer keep still a minute,' he cried indignantly; 'blessed if you don't want lookin' after like a bloomin' kid.'

'I vont to be put down at Sharing Cross,' answered the Frenchman, humbly.

'You vont to be put down at Sharing Cross,' repeated the other bitterly, as he led him back to his seat. 'I shall put yer down in the middle of the road if I 'ave much more of yer. You stop there till I come and sling yer out. I ain't likely to let yer go much past yer Sharing Cross, I shall be too jolly glad to get rid o' yer.'

The poor Frenchman subsided, and we jolted on. At 'The Angel' we, of course, stopped. 'Charing Cross,' shouted the conductor, and up sprang the Frenchman.

'Oh, my Gawd,' said the conductor, taking him by the shoulders and forcing him down into the corner seat, 'wot am I to do? Carn't somebody sit on 'im?'

He held him firmly down until the 'bus started, and then released him. At the top of Chancery Lane the same scene took place, and the poor little Frenchman became exasperated.

'He keep saying Sharing Cross, Sharing Cross,' he exclaimed, turning to the other passengers; 'and it is *no* Sharing Cross. He is fool.'

'Carn't yer understand,' retorted the conductor, equally indignant; 'of course I say Sharing Cross – I mean Charing Cross, but that don't mean that it *is* Charing Cross. That means ——' and then perceiving from the blank look on the Frenchman's face the utter impossibility of ever making the matter clear to him, he turned to us with an appealing gesture, and asked:

'Does any gentleman know the French for "bloomin' idiot?"'

A day or two afterwards, I happened to enter his omnibus again.

'Well,' I asked him, 'did you get your French friend to Charing Cross all right?'

'No, sir,' he replied, 'you'll 'ardly believe it, but I 'ad a bit of a row with a policeman just before I got to the corner, and it put 'im clean out 'o my 'ead. Blessed if I didn't run 'im on to Victoria.'

CHAPTER XI

Said Brown one evening, 'There is but one vice, and that is selfishness.'

Jephson was standing before the fire lighting his pipe. He puffed the tobacco into a glow, threw the match into the embers, and then said:

'And the seed of all virtue also.'

'Sit down and get on with your work,' said MacShaughnassy from the sofa where he lay at full length with his heels on a chair; 'we're discussing the novel. Paradoxes not admitted during business hours.'

Jephson, however, was in an argumentative mood. 'Selfishness,' he continued, 'is merely another name for Will. Every deed, good or bad, that we do is prompted by selfishness. We are charitable to secure ourselves a good place in the next world, to make ourselves respected in this, to ease our own distress at the knowledge of suffering. One man is kind because it gives him pleasure to be kind, just as another is cruel because cruelty pleases him. A great man does his duty because to him the sense of duty done is a deeper delight than would be the ease resulting from avoidance of duty. The religious man is religious because he finds a joy in religion; the moral man moral because with his strong self-respect, viciousness would mean wretchedness. Self-sacrifice itself is only a subtle selfishness: we prefer the mental exaltation gained thereby to the sensual gratification which is the alternative reward. Man cannot be anything else but selfish. Selfishness is the law of all life. Each thing, from the farthest fixed star to the smallest insect crawling on the earth, fighting for itself according to its strength; and brooding over all, the Eternal, working for *Himself:* that is the universe.'

'Have some whisky,' said MacShaughnassy; 'and don't be so complicatedly metaphysical. You make my head ache.'

'If all actions, good and bad, spring from selfishness,' replied Brown, 'then there must be good selfishness and bad selfishness: and your bad selfishness is my plain selfishness, without any adjective, so we are back where we started. I say selfishness – bad selfishness – is the root of all evil, and there you are bound to agree with me.'

'Not always,' persisted Jephson; 'I've known selfishness – selfishness according to the ordinarily accepted meaning of the term – to be productive of good actions. I can give you an instance, if you like.'

'Has it got a moral?' asked MacShaughnassy, drowsily.

Jephson mused a moment. 'Yes,' he said at length; 'a very practical moral – and one very useful to young men.'

'That's the sort of story we want,' said the MacShaughnassy, raising himself into a sitting position. 'You listen to this, Brown.'

Jephson seated himself upon a chair, in his favourite attitude, with his elbows resting upon the back, and smoked for a while in silence.

'There are three people in this story,' he began; 'the wife, the wife's husband, and the other man. In most dramas of this type, it is the wife who is the chief character. In this case, the interesting person is the other man.

'The wife – I met her once: she was the most beautiful woman I have ever seen, and the most wicked-looking; which is saying a good deal for both statements. I remember, during a walking tour one year, coming across a lovely little cottage. It was the sweetest place imaginable. I need not describe it. It was the cottage one sees in pictures, and reads of in sentimental poetry. I was leaning over the neatly-cropped hedge, drinking in its beauty, when at one of the tiny casements I saw, looking out at me, a face. It stayed there only a moment, but in that moment the cottage had become ugly, and I hurried away with a shudder.

'That woman's face reminded me of the incident. It was an angel's face, until the woman herself looked out of it: then you were struck by the strange incongruity between tenement and tenant.

'That at one time she had loved her husband, I have little doubt. Vicious women have few vices, and sordidness is not usually one of them. She had probably married him, borne towards him by one of those waves of passion upon which the souls of animal natures are continually rising and falling. On possession, however, had quickly followed satiety, and from satiety had grown the desire for a new sensation.

'They were living at Cairo at the period; her husband held an important official position there, and by virtue of this, and of her own beauty and tact, her house soon became the centre of the Anglo-Saxon society ever drifting in and out of the city. The women disliked her, and copied her. The men spoke slightingly of her to their wives, lightly of her to each other, and made idiots of themselves when they were alone with her. She laughed at them to their faces, and mimicked them behind their backs. Their friends said it was clever.

'One year there arrived a young English engineer, who had come out to superintend some canal works. He brought with him satisfactory letters of recommendation, and was at once received by the European residents as a welcome addition to their social circle. He was not particularly good-looking, he was not remarkably charming, but he possessed the one thing that few women can resist in a man, and that is strength. The woman looked at the man, and the man looked back at the woman; and the drama began.

'Scandal flies swiftly through small communities. Before a month, their relationship was the chief topic of conversation throughout the quarter. In less than two, it reached the ears of the woman's husband.

'He was either an exceptionally mean or an exceptionally noble character, according to how one views the matter. He worshipped his wife – as men with big hearts and weak brains often do worship such women – with dog-like devotion. His only dread was lest the scandal should reach proportions that would compel him to take notice of it, and thus bring shame and suffering upon the woman to whom he would have given his life. That a man who saw her should love her seemed natural to him; that she should have grown tired of himself, a thing not to be wondered at. He was grateful to her for having once loved him, for a little while.

'She laughed at them'

'As for "the other man," he proved somewhat of an enigma to the gossips. He attempted no secrecy; if anything, he rather paraded his subjugation – or his conquest, it was difficult to decide which term to apply. He rode and drove with her; visited her in public and in private (in such privacy as can be hoped for in a house filled with chattering servants, and watched by spying eyes); loaded her with expensive presents, which she wore openly, and papered his smoking-den with her photographs. Yet he never allowed himself to appear in the least degree ridiculous; never allowed her to come between him and his work. A letter from her, he would lay aside unopened until he had finished what he evidently regarded as more important business. When boudoir and engine-shed became rivals, it was the boudoir that had to wait.

'The woman chafed under his self-control, which stung her like a lash, but clung to him the more abjectly.

'"Tell me you love me!" she would cry fiercely, stretching her white arms towards him.

'"I have told you so," he would reply calmly, without moving.

'"I want to hear you tell it me again," she would plead with a voice that trembled on a sob. "Come close to me and tell it me again, again, again!"

'Then, as she lay with half-closed eyes, he would pour forth a flood of passionate words sufficient to satisfy even her thirsty ears, and afterwards, as the gates clanged behind him, would take up an engineering problem at the exact point at which half an hour before, on her entrance into the room, he had temporarily dismissed it.

'One day, a privileged friend put bluntly to him this question: "Are you playing for love or vanity?"

'To which the man, after long pondering, gave this reply: '"'Pon my soul, Jack, I couldn't tell you."

'Now, when a man is in love with a woman who cannot make up her mind whether she loves him or not, we call the complication comedy; where it is the woman who is in earnest the result is generally tragedy.

'They continued to meet and to make love. They talked – as people in their position are prone to talk – of the beautiful life they would lead if it only were not for the thing that was; of the earthly paradise – or, maybe, "earthy" would be the more suitable adjective – they would each create for the other, if only they had the right which they hadn't.

'She lay with half-closed eyes'

'In this work of imagination the man trusted chiefly to his literary faculties, which were considerable; the woman to her desires. Thus, his scenes possessed a grace and finish which hers lacked, but her pictures were the more vivid. Indeed, so realistic did she paint them, that to herself they seemed realities, waiting for her. Then she would rise to go towards them only to strike herself against the thought of the thing that stood between her and them. At first she only hated the thing, but after a while there came an ugly look of hope into her eyes.

'The time drew near for the man to return to England. The canal was completed, and a day appointed for the letting in of the water. The man determined to make the event the occasion of a social gathering. He invited a large number of guests, among whom were the woman and her husband, to assist at the function. Afterwards the party were to picnic at a pleasant wooded spot some three-quarters of a mile from the first lock.

'The ceremony of flooding was to be performed by the woman, her husband's position entitling her to this distinction. Between the river and the head of the cutting had been left a strong bank of earth, pierced some distance down by a hole, which hole was kept closed by means of a closely-fitting steel plate. The woman drew the lever releasing this plate, and the water rushed through and began to press against the lock gates. When it had attained a certain depth, the sluices were raised, and the water poured down into the deep basin of the lock.

'It was an exceptionally deep lock. The party gathered round and watched the water slowly rising. The woman looked down, and shuddered; the man was standing by her side.

'"How deep it is," she said.

'"Yes," he replied, "it holds thirty feet of water, when full."

'The water crept up inch by inch.

'"Why don't you open the gates, and let it in quickly?" she asked.

'"It would not do for it to come in too quickly," he explained; "we shall half fill this lock, and then open the sluices at the other end, and so let the water pass through."

'The woman looked at the smooth stone walls and at the iron-plated gates.

'"I wonder what a man would do," she said, "if he fell in, and there was no one near to help him?"

'The man laughed. "I think he would stop there," he answered. "Come, the others are waiting for us."

'He lingered a moment to give some final instructions to the workmen. "You can follow on when you've made all right," he said, "and get something to eat. There's no need for more than one to stop." Then they joined the rest of the party, and sauntered on, laughing and talking, to the picnic ground.

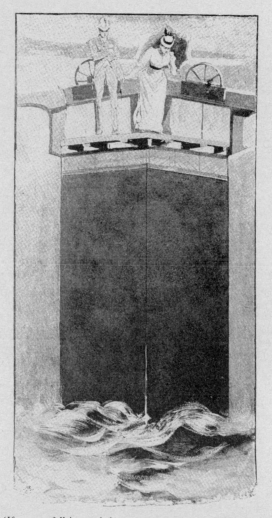

'If a man fell in, and there was no one near to help him?'

'After lunch the party broke up, as is the custom of picnic parties, and wandered away in groups and pairs. The man, whose duty as host had hitherto occupied all his attention, looked for the woman, but she was gone.

'A friend strolled by, the same that had put the question to him about love and vanity.

'"Have you quarrelled?" asked the friend.

'"No," replied the man.

'"I fancied you had," said the other. "I met her just now walking with her husband, of all men in the world, and making herself quite agreeable to him."

'The friend strolled on, and the man sat down on a fallen tree, and lighted a cigar. He smoked and thought, and the cigar burnt out, but he still sat thinking.

'After a while he heard a faint rustling of the branches behind him, and peering between the interlacing leaves that hid him, saw the crouching figure of the woman creeping through the wood.

'His lips were parted to call her name, when she turned her listening head in his direction, and his eyes fell full upon her face. Something about it, he could not have told what, struck him dumb, and the woman crept on.

'Gradually the nebulous thoughts floating through his brain began to solidify into a tangible idea, and the man unconsciously started forward. After walking a few steps he broke into a run, for the idea had grown clearer. It continued to grow still clearer and clearer, and the man ran faster and faster, until at last he found himself racing madly towards the lock. As he approached it he looked round for the watchman who ought to have been there, but the man was gone from his post. He shouted, but if any answer was returned, it was drowned by the roar of the rushing water.

'He reached the edge and looked down. Fifteen feet below him was the reality of the dim vision that had come to him a mile back in the woods: the woman's husband swimming round and round like a rat in a pail.

'The river was flowing in and out of the lock at the same rate, so that the level of the water remained constant. The first thing the man did was to close the lower sluices and then open those in the upper gate to their fullest extent. The water began to rise.

'"Can you hold out?" he cried.

'The drowning man turned to him a face already contorted by the agony of exhaustion, and answered with a feeble "No."

'He looked around for something to throw to the man. A plank had lain there in the morning, he remembered stumbling over it, and complaining of its having been left there; he cursed himself now for his care.

'A hut used by the navvies to keep their tools in stood about two hundred yards away; perhaps it had been taken there, perhaps there he might even find a rope.

'"Just one minute, old fellow!" he shouted down, "and I'll be back."

'But the other did not hear him. The feeble struggles ceased. The face fell back upon the water, the eyes half closed as if with weary indifference. There was no time for him to do more than kick off his riding boots and jump in and clutch the unconscious figure as it sank.

'Down there, in that walled-in trap, he fought a long fight with Death for the life that stood between him and the woman. He was not an expert swimmer, his clothes hampered him, he was already blown with his long race, the burden in his arms dragged him down, the water rose slowly enough to make his torture fit for Dante's hell.

'At first he could not understand why this was so, but in glancing down he saw to his horror that he had not properly closed the lower sluices; in each some eight or ten inches remained open, so that the stream was passing out nearly half as fast as it came in. It would be another five-and-twenty minutes before the water would be high enough for him to grasp the top.

'He noted where the line of wet had reached to, on the smooth stone wall, then looked again after what he thought must be a lapse of ten minutes, and found it had risen half an inch, if that. Once or twice he shouted for help, but the effort taxed severely his already failing breath, and his voice only came back to him in a hundred echoes from his prison walls.

'Inch by inch the line of wet crept up, but the spending of his strength went on more swiftly. It seemed to him as if his inside were being gripped and torn slowly out: his whole body cried out to him to let it sink and lie in rest at the bottom.

'At length his unconscious burden opened its eyes and stared at him stupidly, then closed them again with a sigh; a minute later opened them once more, and looked long and hard at him.

'"Let me go," he said, "we shall both drown. You can manage by yourself."

'He made a feeble effort to release himself, but the other held him.

'"Keep still, you fool!" he hissed; "you're going to get out of this with me, or I'm going down with you."

'So the grim struggle went on in silence, till the man, looking up, saw the stone coping just a little way above his head, made one mad leap and caught it with his finger-tips, held on an instant, then fell back with a "plump" and sank; came up and made another dash, and, helped by the impetus of his rise, caught the coping firmly this time with the whole of his fingers, hung on till his eyes saw the stunted grass, till they were both able to scramble out upon the bank and lie there, their breasts pressed close against the ground, their hands clutching the earth, while the overflowing water swirled softly round them.

'After a while, they raised themselves and looked at one another.

'"Tiring work," said the other man, with a nod towards the lock.

'"Yes," answered the husband, "beastly awkward not being a

good swimmer. How did you know I had fallen in? You met my wife, I suppose?"

'"Yes," said the other man.

'The husband sat staring at a point in the horizon for some minutes. "Do you know what I was wondering this morning?" said he.

'"No," said the other man.

'"Whether I should kill you or not."

'"They told me," he continued, after a pause, "a lot of silly gossip which I was cad enough to believe. I know now it wasn't true, because – well, if it had been, you would not have done what you have done."

'He rose and came across. "I beg your pardon," he said, holding out his hand.

'"I beg yours," said the other man, rising and taking it; "do you mind giving me a hand with the sluices?"

'They set to work to put the lock right.

'"How did you manage to fall in?" asked the other man, who was raising one of the lower sluices, without looking round.

'The husband hesitated, as if he found the explanation somewhat difficult. "Oh," he answered carelessly, "the wife and I were chaffing, and she said she'd often seen you jump it, and" – he laughed a rather forced laugh – "she promised me a – a kiss if I cleared it. It was a foolish thing to do."

'"Yes, it was rather," said the other man.

'A few days afterwards the man and woman met at a reception. He found her in a leafy corner of the garden talking to some friends. She advanced to meet him, holding out her hand. "What can I say more than thank you?" she murmured in a low voice.

'The others moved away, leaving them alone. "They tell me you risked your life to save his?" she said.

'"Yes," he answered.

'She raised her eyes to his, then struck him across the face with her ungloved hand.

'"You damned fool!" she whispered.

'He seized her by her white arms, and forced her back behind the orange trees. "Do you know why?" he said, speaking slowly and distinctly; "because I feared that, with him dead, you would want me to marry you, and that, talked about as we have been, I might find it awkward to avoid doing so; because I feared that, without him to stand between us, you might prove an annoyance to me – perhaps come between me and the woman I love, the woman I am going back to. Now do you understand?"

'"Yes," whispered the woman, and he left her.

'But there are only two people,' concluded Jephson, 'who do not regard his saving of the husband's life as a highly noble and unselfish action, and they are the man himself and the woman.'

We thanked Jephson for his story, and promised to profit by profit by the moral, when discovered. Meanwhile, MacShaughnassy said that he knew a story dealing

'Struck him across the face'

with the same theme, namely, the too close attachment of a woman to a strange man, which really had a moral, which moral was: don't have anything to do with inventions.

Brown, who had patented a safety gun, which he had never yet found a man plucky enough to let off, said it was a bad moral. We agreed to hear the particulars, and judge for ourselves.

'This story,' commenced MacShaughnassy, 'comes from Furtwangen, a small town in the Black Forest. There lived there a very wonderful old fellow named Nicholaus Geibel. His business was the making of mechanical toys, at which work he had acquired an almost European reputation. He made rabbits that would emerge from the heart of a cabbage, flap their ears, smooth their whiskers, and disappear again; cats that would wash their faces, and mew so naturally that dogs would mistake them for real cats, and fly at them; dolls, with phonographs concealed within them, that would raise their hats and say, "Good morning; how do you do?" and some that would even sing a song.

'But he was something more than a mere mechanic; he was an artist. His work was with him a hobby, almost a passion. His shop was filled with all manner of strange things that never would, or could, be sold – things he had made for the pure love of making them. He had contrived a mechanical donkey that would trot for two hours by means of stored electricity, and trot, too, much faster than the live article, and with less need for exertion on the part of the driver; a bird that would shoot up into the air, fly round and round in a circle, and drop to earth at the exact spot from where it started; a skeleton that, supported by an upright iron bar, would dance a hornpipe; a life-size lady doll that could play the fiddle; and a gentleman with a hollow inside who could smoke a pipe and drink more lager beer than any three average German students put together, which is saying much.

'Indeed, it was the belief of the town that old Geibel could make a man capable of doing everything that a respectable man need want to do. One day he made a man who did too much, and it came about in this way.

'Young Doctor Follen had a baby, and the baby had a birthday. Its first birthday put Doctor Follen's household into somewhat of a flurry, but on the occasion of its second birthday, Mrs Doctor Follen gave a ball in honour of the event. Old Geibel and his daughter Olga were among the guests.

'During the afternoon of the next day, some three or four of Olga's bosom friends, who had also been present at the ball, dropped in to have a chat about it. They naturally fell to discussing the men, and to criticising their dancing. Old Geibel was in the room, but he appeared to be absorbed in his newspaper, and the girls took no notice of him.

'"There seem to be fewer men who can dance, at every ball you go to," said one of the girls.

'"Yes, and don't the ones who can, give themselves airs," said another; "they make quite a favour of asking you."

'"And how stupidly they talk," added a third. "They always say exactly the same things: 'How charming you are looking to-night.' 'Do you often go to Vienna?' 'Oh, you should, it's delightful.' 'What a charming dress you have on.' 'What a warm day it has been.' 'Do you like Wagner?' I do wish they'd think of something new."

'"Oh, I never mind how they talk," said a fourth. "If a man dances well he may be a fool for all I care."

'"He generally is," slipped in a thin girl, rather spitefully.

'"I go to a ball to dance," continued the previous speaker, not noticing the interruption. "All I ask of a partner is that he shall hold me firmly, take me round steadily, and not get tired before I do."

'"A clockwork figure would be the thing for you," said the girl who had interrupted.

'"Bravo!" cried one of the others, clapping her hands, "what a capital idea!"

'"What's a capital idea?" they asked.

'"Why, a clockwork dancer, or, better still, one that would go by electricity and never run down."

'The girls took up the idea with enthusiasm.

'"Oh, what a lovely partner he would make," said one; "he would never kick you, or tread on your toes."

'"Or tear your dress," said another.

'"Or get out of step."

'"Or get giddy and lean on you."

'"And he would never want to mop his face with his handkerchief. I do hate to see a man do that after every dance."

'"And wouldn't want to spend the whole evening in the supper-room."

'"Why, with a phonograph inside him to grind out all the stock remarks, you would not be able to tell him from a real man," said the girl who had first suggested the idea.

'"Oh yes, you would," said the thin girl, "he would be so much nicer."

'Old Geibel had laid down his paper, and was listening with both his ears. On one of the girls glancing in his direction, however, he hurriedly hid himself again behind it.

'After the girls were gone, he went into his workshop, where Olga heard him walking up and down, and every now and then chuckling to himself; and that night he talked to her a good deal about dancing and dancing men –

'What steps were gone through'

'For a couple of weeks he kept to his factory'

asked what they usually said and did – what dances were most popular – what steps were gone through, with many other questions bearing on the subject.

'Then for a couple of weeks he kept much to his factory, and was very thoughtful and busy, though prone at unexpected moments to break into a quiet low laugh, as if enjoying a joke that nobody else knew of.

'A month later another ball took place in Furtwangen. On this occasion it was given by old Wenzel, the wealthy timber merchant, to celebrate his niece's betrothal, and Geibel and his daughter were again among the invited.

'When the hour arrived to set out, Olga sought her father. Not finding him in the house, she tapped at the door of his workshop. He appeared in his shirt-sleeves, looking hot, but radiant.

'"Don't wait for me," he said, "you go on, I'll follow you. I've got something to finish."

'As she turned to obey he called after her, "Tell them I'm going to bring a young man with me – such a nice young man, and an excellent dancer. All the girls will like him." Then he laughed and closed the door.

'Her father generally kept his doings secret from everybody, but she had a pretty shrewd suspicion of what he had been planning, and so, to a certain extent, was able to prepare the guests for what was coming. Anticipation ran high, and the arrival of the famous mechanist was eagerly awaited.

'At length the sound of wheels was heard outside, followed by a great commotion in the passage, and old Wenzel himself, his jolly face red with excitement and suppressed laughter, burst into the room and announced in stentorian tones:

'"Herr Geibel – and a friend."

'Herr Geibel and his "friend" entered, greeted with shouts of laughter and applause, and advanced to the centre of the room.

'"Allow me, ladies and gentlemen," said Herr Geibel, "to introduce you to my friend, Lieutenant Fritz. Fritz, my dear fellow, bow to the ladies and gentlemen."

'Geibel placed his hand encouragingly on Fritz's shoulder, and the lieutenant bowed low, accompanying the action with a harsh clicking noise in his throat, unpleasantly suggestive of a death rattle. But that was only a detail.

'"He walks a little stiffly" (old Geibel took his arm and walked him forward a few steps. He certainly did walk stiffly), "but then, walking is not his forte. He is essentially a dancing man. I have only been able to teach him the waltz as yet, but at that he is faultless. Come, which of you ladies may I introduce

'My friend, Lieutenant Fritz'

him to, as a partner? He keeps perfect time; he never gets tired; he won't kick you or tread on your dress; he will hold you as firmly as you like, and go as quickly or as slowly as you please; he never gets giddy; and he is full of conversation. Come, speak up for yourself, my boy."

'The old gentleman twisted one of the buttons of his coat, and immediately Fritz opened his mouth and in thin tones that appeared to proceed from the back of his head, remarked suddenly, "May I have the pleasure?" and then shut his mouth again with a snap.

'That Lieutenant Fritz had made a strong impression on the company was undoubted, yet none of the girls seemed inclined to dance with him. They looked askance at his waxen face, with its staring eyes and fixed smile, and shuddered. At last old Geibel came to the girl who had conceived the idea.

'"It is your own suggestion, carried out to the letter," said Geibel, "an electric dancer. You owe it to the gentleman to give him a trial."

'She was a bright saucy little girl, fond of a frolic. Her host added his entreaties, and she consented.

'Herr Geibel fixed the figure to her. Its right arm was screwed round her waist, and held her firmly; its delicately jointed left hand was made to fasten itself upon her right. The old toymaker showed her how to regulate its speed, and how to stop it, and release herself.

'"It will take you round in a complete circle," he explained; "be careful that no one knocks against you, and alters its course."

'The music struck up. Old Geibel put the current in motion, and Annette and her strange partner began to dance.

'For a while every one stood watching them. The figure performed its purpose admirably. Keeping perfect time and step, and holding its little partner tightly clasped in an unyielding embrace, it revolved steadily, pouring forth at the same time a constant flow of squeaky conversation, broken by brief intervals of grinding silence.

'"How charming you are looking to-night," it remarked in its thin, far-away voice. "What a lovely day it has been. Do you like dancing? How well our steps agree. You will give me another, won't you? Oh, don't be so cruel. What a charming gown you have on. Isn't waltzing delightful? I could go on dancing for ever – with you. Have you had supper?"

'As she grew more familiar with the uncanny creature, the girls' nervousness wore off, and she entered into the fun of the thing.

'"Oh, he's just lovely," she cried, laughing, "I could go on dancing with him all my life."

'Couple after couple now joined them, and soon all the

216

dancers in the room were whirling round behind them. Nicholaus Geibel stood looking on, beaming with childish delight at his success.

'Old Wenzel approached him, and whispered something in his ear. Geibel laughed and nodded, and the two worked their way quietly towards the door.

'"This is the young people's house to-night," said Wenzel, as soon as they were outside; "you and I will have a quiet pipe and a glass of hock, over in the counting-house."

'Meanwhile the dancing grew more fast and furious. Little Annette loosened the screw regulating her partner's rate of progress, and the figure flew round with her swifter and swifter. Couple after couple dropped out exhausted, but they only went the faster, till at length they were the only pair left dancing.

'Madder and madder became the waltz. The music lagged behind: the musicians, unable to keep pace, ceased, and sat staring. The younger guests applauded, but the older faces began to grow anxious.

'"Hadn't you better stop, dear," said one of the women, "you'll make yourself so tired."

'But Annette did not answer.

'"I believe she's fainted," cried out a girl, who had caught sight of her face as it was swept by.

'One of the men sprang forward and clutched at the figure, but its impetus threw him down on to the floor, where its steel-cased feet laid bare his cheek. The thing evidently did not intend to part with its prize easily.

'Had any one retained a cool head, the figure, one cannot help thinking, might easily have been stopped. Two or three men, acting in concert, might have lifted it bodily off the floor, or have jammed it into a corner. But few human heads are capable of remaining cool under excitement. Those who are not present think how stupid must have been those who were; those who are, reflect afterwards how simple it would have been to do this, that or the other, if only they had thought of it at the time.

'The women grew hysterical. The men shouted contradictory directions to one another. Two of them made a bungling rush at the figure, which had the result of forcing it out of its orbit in the centre of the room, and sending it crashing against the walls and furniture. A stream of blood showed itself down the girl's white frock, and followed her along the floor. The affair was becoming horrible. The women rushed screaming from the room. The men followed them.

'One sensible suggestion was made: "Find Geibel – fetch Geibel."

'No one had noticed him leave the room, no one knew where he was. A party went in search of him. The others, too unnerved to go back into the ball-room, crowded outside the door and listened. They could hear the steady whir of the wheels upon the polished floor, as the thing spun round and round; the dull thud as every now and again it dashed itself and its burden against some opposing object and ricocheted off in a new direction.

'And everlastingly it talked in that thin ghostly voice, repeating over and over the same formula: "How charming you are looking to-night. What a lovely day it has been. Oh, don't be so cruel. I could go on dancing for ever – with you. Have you had supper?"

'Of course they sought for Geibel everywhere but where he was. They looked in every room in the house, then they rushed off in a body to his own place, and spent precious minutes in waking up his deaf old housekeeper. At last it occurred to one of the party that Wenzel was missing also, and then the idea of the counting-house across the yard presented itself to them, and there they found him.

'He rose up, very pale and followed them; and he and old Wenzel forced their way through the crowd of guests gathered outside, and entered the room, and locked the door behind them.

'From within there came the muffled sound of low voices and quick steps, followed by a confused scuffling noise, then silence, then the low voices again.

'After a time the door opened, and those near it pressed forward to enter, but old Wenzel's broad shoulders barred the way.

'"I want you – and you, Bekler," he said, addressing a couple of the elder men. His voice was calm, but his face was deadly white. "The rest of you, please go – get the women away as quickly as you can."

'From that day old Nicholaus Geibel confined himself to the making of mechanical rabbits and cats that mewed and washed their faces.'

We agreed that the moral of MacShaughnassy's story was a good one.

CHAPTER XII

How much more of our – fortunately not very valuable – time we devoted to this wonderful novel of ours, I cannot exactly say. Turning the dogs'-eared leaves of the dilapidated diary that lies before me, I find the record of our later gatherings confused and incomplete. For weeks there does not appear a single word. Then comes an alarmingly business-like minute of a meeting at which there was – 'Present: Jephson, MacShaughnassy, Brown, and Self'; and at which the 'Proceedings commenced at 8.30.' At what time the 'proceedings' terminated, and what business was done, the chronicle, however, sayeth not; though, faintly pencilled in the margin of the page, I trace these hieroglyphics: '3.14.9 – 2.6.7,' bringing out a result of '1.8.2.' Evidently an unremunerative night.

On September 13th we seem to have become suddenly imbued with energy to a quite remarkable degree, for I read that we 'Resolved to start the first chapter at once' – 'at once' being underlined. After this spurt, we rest until October 4th, when we 'Discussed whether it should be a novel of plot or of character,' without – so far as the diary affords indication – arriving at any definite decision. I observe that on the same day 'Mac told a story about a man who accidentally bought a camel at a sale.' Details of the story are, however, wanting, which, perhaps, is fortunate for the reader.

On the 16th, we were still debating the character of our hero; and I see that I suggested 'a man of the Charley Buswell type.'

Poor Charley, I wonder what could have made me think of him in connection with heroes; his lovableness, I suppose –

certainly not his heroic qualities. I can recall his boyish face now (it was always a boyish face), the tears streaming down it as he sat in the schoolyard beside a bucket, in which he was drowning three white mice and a tame rat. I sat down opposite and cried too, while helping him to hold a saucepan lid over the poor little creatures, and thus there sprang up a friendship between us, which grew.

Over the grave of these murdered rodents, he took a solemn oath never to break school rules again, by keeping either white mice or tame rats, but to devote the whole of his energies for the future to pleasing his masters, and affording his parents some satisfaction for the money being spent upon his education.

Seven weeks later, the pervadence throughout the dormitory of an atmospheric effect more curious than pleasing led to the discovery that he had converted his box into a rabbit hutch. Confronted with eleven kicking witnesses, and reminded of his former promises, he explained that rabbits were not mice, and seemed to consider that a new and vexatious regulation had been sprung upon him. The rabbits were confiscated. What was their ultimate fate, we never knew with certainty, but three days later we were given rabbit-pie for dinner. To comfort him I endeavoured to assure him that these could not be his rabbits. He, however, convinced that they were, cried steadily into his plate all the time that he was eating them, and afterwards, in the playgound, had a stand-up fight with a fourth form boy who had requested a second helping.

That evening he performed another solemn oath-taking, and for the next month was the model boy of the school. He read tracts, sent his spare pocket-money to assist in annoying the heathen, and subscribed to *The Young Christian* and *The Weekly Rambler*, an Evangelical Miscellany (whatever that may mean). An undiluted course of this pernicious literature naturally created in him a desire towards the opposite extreme. He suddenly dropped *The Young Christian* and *The Weekly*

Rambler, and purchased penny dreadfuls; and taking no further interest in the welfare of the heathen, saved up and bought a second-hand revolver and a hundred cartridges. His ambition, he confided to me, was to become 'a dead shot,' and the marvel of it is that he did not succeed.

Of course, there followed the usual discovery and consequent trouble, the usual repentance and reformation, the usual determination to start a new life.

Poor fellow, he lived 'starting a new life.' Every New Year's Day he would start a new life – on his birthday – on other people's birthdays. I fancy that, later on, when he came to know their importance, he extended the principle to quarter days. 'Tidying up, and starting afresh,' he always called it.

I think as a young man he was better than most of us. But he lacked that great gift which is the distinguishing feature of the English-speaking race all the world over, the gift of hypocrisy. He seemed incapable of doing the slightest thing without getting found out; a grave misfortune for a man to suffer from, this.

Dear simple-hearted fellow, it never occurred to him that he was as other men – with, perhaps, a dash of straightforwardness added; he regarded himself as a monster of depravity. One evening I found him in his chambers engaged upon his Sisyphean labour of 'tidying up.' A heap of letters, photographs, and bills lay before him. He was tearing them up and throwing them into the fire.

I came towards him, but he stopped me. 'Don't come near me,' he cried, 'don't touch me. I'm not fit to shake hands with a decent man.'

It was the sort of speech to make one feel hot and uncomfortable. I did not know what to answer, and murmured something about his being no worse than the average.

'Don't talk like that,' he answered excitedly; 'you say that to comfort me, I know; but I don't like to hear it. If I thought other men were like me I should be ashamed of being a man.

I've been a blackguard, old fellow, but, please God, it's not too late. To-morrow morning I begin a new life.'

He finished his work of destruction, and then rang the bell, and sent his man downstairs for a bottle of champagne.

'My last drink,' he said, as we clicked glasses. 'Here's to the old life out, and the new life in.'

He took a sip and flung the glass with the remainder into the fire. He was always a little theatrical, especially when most in earnest.

For a long while after that I saw nothing of him. Then, one evening, sitting down to supper at a restaurant, I noticed him opposite to me in company that could hardly be called doubtful.

He flushed and came over to me. 'I've been an old woman for nearly six months,' he said, with a laugh. 'I find I can't stand it any longer.'

'After all,' he continued, 'what is life for but to live? It's only hypocritical to try and be a thing we are not. And do you know' – he leant across the table, speaking earnestly – 'honestly and seriously, I'm a better man – I feel it and know it – when I am my natural self than when I am trying to be an impossible saint.'

That was the mistake he made; he always ran to extremes. He thought that an oath, if it were only big enough, would frighten away Human Nature, instead of serving only as a challenge to it. Accordingly, each reformation was more intemperate than the last, to be duly followed by a greater swing of the pendulum in the opposite direction.

Being now in a thoroughly reckless mood, he went the pace rather hotly. Then, one evening, without any previous warning, I had a note from him. 'Come round and see me on Thursday. It is my wedding eve.'

I went. He was once more 'tidying up.' All his drawers were open, and on the table were piled packs of cards, betting books, and much written paper, all, as before, in course of demolition.

I smiled: I could not help it, and, no way abashed, he laughed his usual hearty, honest laugh.

'I know,' he exclaimed gaily, 'but this is not the same as the others.'

Then, laying his hand on my shoulder, and speaking with the sudden seriousness that comes so readily to shallow natures, he said, 'God has heard my prayer, old friend. He knows I am weak. He has sent down an angel out of Heaven to help me.'

He took her portrait from the mantelpiece and handed it to me. It seemed to me the face of a hard, narrow woman, but, of course, he raved about her.

As he talked, there fluttered to the ground from the heap before him an old restaurant bill, and, stooping, he picked it up and held it in his hand, musing.

'Have you ever noticed how the scent of the champagne and the candles seems to cling to these things?' he said lightly, sniffing carelessly at it. 'I wonder what's become of her?'

'I think I wouldn't think about her at all to-night,' I answered.

He loosened his hand, letting the paper fall into the fire.

'My God!' he cried vehemently, 'when I think of all the wrong I have done – the irreparable, ever-widening ruin I have perhaps brought into the world – O God! spare me a long life that I may make amends. Every hour, every minute of it shall be devoted to your service.'

As he stood there, with his eager boyish eyes upraised, a light seemed to fall upon his face and illumine it. I had pushed the photograph back to him, and it lay upon the table before him. He knelt and pressed his lips to it.

'With your help, my darling, and His,' he murmured.

The next morning he was married. She was a well-meaning girl, though her piety, as is the case with most people, was of the negative order; and her antipathy to things evil much stronger than her sympathy with things good. For a longer time than I had expected she kept him straight – perhaps a little too straight. But at last there came the inevitable relapse.

I called upon him, in answer to an excited message, and found him in the depths of despair. It was the old story, human weakness, combined with lamentable lack of the most ordinary precautions against being found out. He gave me details, interspersed with exuberant denunciations of himself, and I undertook the delicate task of peace-maker.

It was a weary work, but eventually she consented to forgive him. His joy, when I told him, was boundless.

'How good women are,' he said, while the tears came into his eyes. 'But she shall not repent it. Please God, from this day forth, I'll ——'

He stopped, and for the first time in his life the doubt of himself crossed his mind. As I sat watching him, the joy died out of his face, and the first hint of age passed over it.

'I seem to have been "tidying up and starting afresh" all my life,' he said wearily; 'I'm beginning to see where the untidiness lies, and the only way to get rid of it.'

I did not understand the meaning of his words at the time, but learnt it later on.

He strove, according to his strength, and fell. But by a miracle his transgression was not discovered. The facts came to light long afterwards, but at the time there were only two who knew.

It was his last failure. Late one evening I received a hurriedly-scrawled note from his wife, begging me to come round.

'A terrible thing has happened,' it ran; 'Charley went up to his study after dinner, saying he had some "tidying up," as he calls it, to do, and did not wish to be disturbed. In clearing out his desk he must have handled carelessly the revolver that he always keeps there, not remembering, I suppose, that it was loaded. We heard a report, and on rushing into the room found him lying dead on the floor. The bullet had passed right through his heart.'

Hardly the type of man for a hero! And yet I do not know. Perhaps he fought harder than many a man who conquers. In the world's courts, we are compelled to judge on circumstantial evidence only, and the chief witness, the man's soul, cannot very well be called.

I remember the subject of bravery being discussed one evening at a dinner party, when a German gentleman present related an anecdote, the hero of which was a young Prussian officer.

'I cannot give you his name,' our German friend explained – 'the man himself told me the story in confidence; and though he personally, by virtue of his after record, could afford to have it known, there are other reasons why it should not be bruited about.

'How I learnt it was in this way. For a dashing exploit performed during the brief war against Austria he had been presented with the Iron Cross. This, as you are well aware, is the most highly-prized decoration in our army; men who have earned it are usually conceited about it, and, indeed, have some excuse for being so. He, on the contrary, kept his locked in a drawer of his desk, and never wore it except when compelled by official etiquette. The mere sight of it seemed to be painful to him. One day I asked him the reason. We are very old and close friends, and he told me.

'The incident occurred when he was a young lieutenant. Indeed, it was his first engagement. By some means or another he had become separated from his company, and, unable to regain it, had attached himself to a line regiment stationed at the extreme right of the Prussian lines.

'The enemy's effort was mainly directed against the left centre, and for a while our young lieutenant was nothing more than a distant spectator of the battle. Suddenly, however, the attack shifted, and the regiment found itself occupying an extremely important and critical position. The shells began to fall unpleasantly near, and the order was given to "grass."

'The men fell upon their faces and waited. The shells ploughed the ground around them, smothering them with dirt. A horrible, griping pain started in my young friend's stomach, and began creeping upwards. His head and heart both seemed to be shrinking and growing cold. A shot tore off the head of the man next to him, sending the blood spurting into his face; a minute later another ripped upon the back of a poor fellow lying to the front of him.

'His body seemed not to belong to himself at all. A strange, shrivelled creature had taken possession of it. He raised his head and peered about him. He and three soldiers – youngsters, like himself, who had never before been under fire – appeared to be utterly alone in that hell. They were the end men of the regiment, and the configuration of the ground completely hid them from their comrades.

'They glanced at each other, these four, and read one another's thoughts. Leaving their rifles lying on the grass, they commenced to crawl stealthily upon their bellies, the lieutenant leading, the other three following.

'Some few hundred yards in front of them rose a small, steep hill. If they could reach this it would shut them out of

'Commenced to crawl stealthily'

sight. They hastened on, pausing every thirty yards or so to lie still and pant for breath, then hurrying on again, quicker than before, tearing their flesh against the broken ground.

'At last they reached the base of the slope, and slinking a little way round it, raised their heads and looked back. Where they were it was impossible for them to be seen from the Prussian lines.

'They sprang to their feet and broke into a wild race. A dozen steps further they came face to face with an Austrian field battery.

'The demon that had taken possession of them had been growing stronger the further they had fled. They were not men, they were animals mad with fear. Driven by the same frenzy that prompted other panic-stricken creatures to once rush down a steep place into the sea, these four men, with a yell, flung themselves, sword in hand, upon the whole battery; and the whole battery, bewildered by the suddenness and unexpectedness of the attack, thinking the entire battalion was upon them, gave way, and rushed pell-mell down the hill.

'With the sight of those flying Austrians the fear, as independently as it had come to him, left him, and he felt only a desire to hack and kill. The four Prussians flew after them, cutting and stabbing at them as they ran; and when the Prussian cavalry came thundering up, they found my young lieutenant and his three friends had captured two guns and accounted for half a score of the enemy.

'Next day, he was summoned to headquarters.

'"Will you be good enough to remember for the future, sir," said the Chief of the Staff, "that His Majesty does not require his lieutenants to execute manoeuvres on their own responsibility, and also that to attack a battery with three men is not war, but damned tomfoolery. You ought to be court-martialled, sir!"

'Then, in somewhat different tones, the old soldier added, his face softening into a smile: "However, alertness and daring, my young friend, are good qualities, especially when crowned with success. If the Austrians had once succeeded in planting a battery on that hill it might have been difficult to dislodge them. Perhaps, under the circumstances, His Majesty may overlook your indiscretion."

"'His Majesty not only overlooked it, but bestowed upon me the Iron Cross," concluded my friend. "For the credit of the army, I judged it better to keep quiet and take it. But, as you can understand, the sight of it does not recall very pleasurable reflection."'

To return to my diary, I see that on November 14th we held another meeting. But at this there were present only 'Jephson, MacShaughnassy, and Self'; and of Brown's name I find henceforth no further trace. On Christmas eve we three met again, and my notes inform me that MacShaughnassy brewed some whiskey-punch, according to a recipe of his own, a record suggestive of a sad Christmas for all three of us. No particular business appears to have been accomplished on either occasion.

Then there is a break until February 8th, and the assemblage has shrunk to 'Jephson and Self.' With a final flicker, as of a dying candle, my diary at this point, however, grows luminous, shedding much light upon that evening's conversation.

Our talk seems to have been of many things – of most things, in fact, except our novel. Among other subjects we spoke of literature generally.

'I am tired of this eternal cackle about books,' said Jephson; 'these columns of criticism to every line of writing; these endless books about books; these shrill praises and shrill denunciations; this silly worship of novelist Tom; this silly hate of poet Dick; this silly squabbling over playwright Harry. There is no soberness, no sense in it all. One would think, to listen to the High Priests of Culture, that man was made for literature, not literature for man. Thought existed before the Printing Press; and the men who wrote the best hundred books never read them. Books have their place in the world, but they are not its purpose. They are things side by side with beef and mutton, the scent of the sea, the touch of a hand, the memory of a hope, and all the other items in the sum-total of our three-score years and ten. Yet we speak of them as though they were the voice of Life instead of merely its faint echo. Tales are delightful *as* tales – sweet as primroses after the long winter, restful as the cawing of rooks at sunset. But we do not write "tales" now; we prepare "human documents" and dissect souls.'

He broke off abruptly in the midst of his tirade. 'Do you know what these "psychological studies," that are so fashionable just now, always make me think of?' he said. 'One monkey examining another monkey for fleas.'

'And what, after all, does our dissecting pen lay bare?' he continued. 'Human nature? or merely some more or less unsavoury undergarment, disguising and disfiguring human nature? There is a story told of an elderly tramp, who, overtaken by misfortune, was compelled to retire for a while to the seclusion of Portland. His hosts, desiring to see as much as possible of their guest during his limited stay with them, proceeded to bath him. They bathed him twice a day for a week, each time learning more of him; until at last they reached a flannel shirt. And with that they had to be content, soap and water proving powerless to go further.

'That tramp appears to me symbolical of mankind. Human Nature has worn its conventions for so long that its habit has grown on to it. In this nineteenth century it is impossible to say where the clothes of custom end and the natural man begins. Our virtues are taught to us as a branch of "Deportment"; our vices are the recognised vices of our reign and set. Our religion hangs ready-made beside our cradle to be buttoned upon us by loving hands. Our tastes we acquire, with difficulty; our sentiments we learn by rote. At cost of infinite suffering, we study to love whiskey and cigars, high art and classical music. In one age we admire Byron and drink sweet champagne: twenty years later it is more fashionable to prefer Shelley, and we like our champagne dry. At school we are told that Shakespeare is a great poet, and that the Venus di Medici is a fine piece of sculpture; and so for the rest of our lives we go about saying what a great poet we think Shakespeare, and that there is no piece of sculpture, in our opinion, so fine as the Venus di Medici. If we are Frenchmen we adore our mother; if

'You must be mad'

Englishmen we love dogs and virtue. We grieve for the death of a near relative twelve months; but for a second cousin we sorrow only three. The good man has his regulation excellencies to strive after, his regulation sins to repent of. I knew a good man who was quite troubled because he was not proud, and could not, therefore, with any reasonableness, pray for humility. In society one must needs be cynical and mildly wicked: in Bohemia, orthodoxly unorthodox. I remember my mother expostulating with a friend, and actress, who had left a devoted husband and eloped with a disagreeable, ugly, little low comedian (I am speaking of long, long ago).

'"You must be mad," said my mother; "what on earth induced you to take such a step?"

'"My dear Emma," replied the lady; "what else was there for me? You know I can't act. I had to do *something* to show I was an artiste!"

'We are dressed-up marionettes. Our voice is the voice of the unseen showman, Convention; our very movements of passion and pain are but in answer to his jerk. A man resembles one of those gigantic bundles that one sees in nursemaids' arms. It is very bulky and very long; it looks a mass of delicate lace and rich fur and fine woven stuffs; and somewhere, hidden out of sight among the finery, there is a tiny red bit of bewildered humanity, with no voice but a foolish cry.

'There is but one story,' he went on, after a long pause, uttering his own thoughts aloud rather than speaking to me. 'We sit at our desks and think and think, and write and write, but the story is ever the same. Men told it and men listened to it many years ago; we are telling it to one another a thousand years hence; and the story is: "Once upon a time there lived a man, and a woman who loved him." The little critic cries that it is not new, and asks for something fresh, thinking – as children do – that there are strange things in the world.'

At that point my notes end, and there is nothing in the book beyond. Whether any of us thought any more of the novel, whether we ever met again to discuss it, whether it were ever begun, whether it were ever abandoned – I cannot say. There is a fairy story that I read many, many years ago that has never ceased to haunt me. It told how a little boy once climbed a rainbow. And at the end of the rainbow, just behind the clouds, he found a wondrous city. Its houses were of gold, and its streets were paved with silver, and the light that shone upon it was as the light that lies upon the sleeping world at dawn. In this city there were palaces so beautiful that merely to look upon them satisfied all desires; temples so perfect that they who once knelt therein were cleansed of sin. And all the men who dwelt in this wondrous city were great and good, and the women fairer than the women of a young man's dreams. And the name of the city was, 'The city of the things men meant to do.'